SAFER SEX IN PERSONAL RELATIONSHIPS

The Role of Sexual Scripts in
HIV Infection and Prevention

LEA's Series on Personal Relationships
Steve Duck, Series Editor

SAFER SEX IN PERSONAL RELATIONSHIPS

The Role of Sexual Scripts in HIV Infection and Prevention

TARA M. EMMERS-SOMMER
University of Arizona

MIKE ALLEN
University of Wisconsin-Milwaukee

LAWRENCE ERLBAUM ASSOCIATES, PUBLISHERS
2005   Mahwah, New Jersey   London

Lawrence Erlbaum Associates, Inc., Publishers
10 Industrial Avenue
Mahwah, New Jersey 07430

Cover design by Kathryn Houghtaling Lacey

Library of Congress Cataloging-in-Publication Data

Emmers-Sommer, Tara M.
    Safer sex in personal relationships : the role of sexual scripts in HIV infection and prevention / Tara M. Emmers-Sommer, Mike Allen.
        p.   cm. (LEA's series on personal relationships)
    Includes bibliographical references and index.
ISBN 0-8058-4446-5 (cloth : alk. Paper)
    1. Safe sex in AIDS prevention. 2. Couples—Sexual behavior. 3. Interpersonal relations. I. Allen, Mike, 1959– II. Title. III. Series.

HQ21.E64 2005
613.9'5—dc22   2004053201
                                                                          CIP

Books published by Lawrence Erlbaum Associates are printed on acid-free paper, and their bindings are chosen for strength and durability.

Printed in the United States of America
10 9 8 7 6 5 4 3 2 1

Contents

LEA's Series on Personal Relationships

Steve Duck, Series Editor
University of Iowa

Since its inception, the Personal Relationships series from Lawrence Erlbaum Associates has sought to review the progress in the academic work on relationships with respect to a broad array of issues and to do so in an accessible manner that also illustrates its practical value. The LEA series includes books intended to pass on the accumulated scholarship to the next generation of students and to those who deal with relationship issues in the broader world beyond the academy. The series comprises not only monographs and other academic resources exemplifying the multidisciplinary nature of this area, but also books suitable for use in the growing numbers of courses on relationships.

The series has the goal of providing a comprehensive and current survey of theory and research in personal relationships through the careful analysis of the problems encountered and solved in research, yet it also considers the systematic application of that work in a practical context. These resources not only are intended to be comprehensive assessments of progress on particular "hot" and relevant topics, but also will be significant influences on the future directions and development of the study of personal relationships. Although each volume is focused, authors place their respective topics in the broader context of other research on relationships and within a range of wider disciplinary traditions. The series already offers incisive and forward-looking reviews and also demonstrates the broader theoretical implications of relationships for the range of disciplines from which the research originates. Present and future volumes include original studies, reviews of relevant theory and research, and new theories oriented toward the understanding of personal relationships both in themselves and within the context of broader theories of family process, social psychology, and communication.

Reflecting the diverse composition of personal relationship study, readers in numerous disciplines—social psychology, communication, sociology, family studies, developmental psychology, clinical psychology, personality, counseling, women's studies, gerontology, and others—will find valuable and insightful perspectives in the series.

Apart from the academic scholars who research the dynamics and processes of relationships, there are many other people whose work involves them in the operation of relationships in the real world. For such people as nurses, police, teachers, therapists, lawyers, drug and alcohol counselors, marital counselors, and those who take care of the elderly, a number of issues routinely arise concerning the ways in which relationships affect the people whom they serve. Examples of these are: the role of loneliness in illness and the ways to circumvent it; the complex impact of family and peer relationships on a drug-dependent person's attempts to give up the drug; the role of playground unpopularity on a child's learning; the issues involved in dealing with the relational side of chronic illness; the management of conflict in marriage; the establishment of good rapport between physicians and seriously ill patients; the support of the bereaved; and the correction of violent styles of behavior in dating or marriage. Each of these is a problem that may confront some of these professionals as part of their daily concerns and each demonstrates the far-reaching influences of relationship processes in one's life that is presently theorized independently of relationship considerations.

The present volume follows these precepts and invokes the notion that relational communication is a health-related activity. This is true not only in respect of scripts enacted and developed for individuals in personal relationships but also as regards the personal dilemmas and predicaments that present themselves in those relationships as a result of health concerns (for example, the difficulties of negotiating condom use when each partner is supposed to trust one another and a trusting person would not question the other person's cleanness. The issue of trust runs broadly through personal relationships and in this context its negotiation has many ramifications that the book unfolds for us).

A number of other issues in the conduct of sexuality within personal relationships are also given deep consideration here, whether in heterosexual or homosexual personal relationships. These concern such factors as timing of discussion about sexual diseases (where early mention of the topics might scare off a potential partner), social norms (such as the rule that you do not kiss and tell about previous partners or their sexual conditions), personal privacy, and the awkwardness associated with any discussions about sexual activity. Complications arise here when the partners in long-term committed relationships are in the 15 to 25% of folks who have not have been completely faithful to one another (see the Dunscombe et al., book on marital affairs, also in this series), because any extramarital activity brings the risks of exposure to sexually transmitted diseases transported into the relationship.

The book is also forthright in considering the elderly population, which is by no means exempt from the risks of sexually transmitted disease. Here also the existing research on relationships has something to contribute to the understanding of best practices with respect to avoidance or management of sexually transmitted disease.

If these topics were not enough to show the relevance of relationships to disease, the book considers the community results of individual relational practices and the ways in which communities of relational networks assume responsibility for the management and care of those with serious sexually transmitted diseases such as AIDS. AIDS does not occur only to an individual but also to a community and the book reports research and practical issues that arise from this circumstance.

Preface

HIV and AIDS are global issues that affect us all—not only socially, but culturally, economically, medically, politically, interpersonally, and personally. Many individuals perceive themselves as removed from or immune to HIV and/or AIDS. In some form or another, however, one will be touched and affected by HIV and/or AIDS. The announcement in July of 2004 that the world is losing the fight against HIV infection is sobering—38 million people infected, and 4.8 million new cases expected in 2004 with 3 million persons dying of ARC. The issues of education and prevention have become more important, now more than ever.

Many existing studies on HIV and AIDS approach the phenomenon from a medical standpoint or a largely social standpoint. We applaud these efforts and encourage further works in these domains to increase awareness and understanding of HIV and AIDS. We noticed, however, that much of the extant research was remiss in terms of approaching HIV and AIDS from an interpersonal/personal perspective. Being communication scholars, we were surprised to learn that, although discussions regarding sexual histories, sexual practices, safer sex behavior, and condom use are interpersonal communication phenomena, little existed in the extant literature on the tremendous role that communication has in the discussion and practice of safer sex. Similarly, we noticed that much of the existing research focused heavily on homosexuals or men having sex with men (MSM) and paid less attention to relationship types that also carried potential risk. For example, relationships involving aged or married partners, or with cultural or intercultural components, remain understudied in the literature, but are no less important. Our purpose in writing this book is to approach HIV and AIDS in a variety of close relationship types from an interpersonal, communication perspective. Our goal is to be both theoretical and practical. To accomplish this objective, script theory from a developmental perspective serves as the primary theoretical framework of the book, with related theories subsumed. In addition, we offer practical, prescriptive information that we hope will resonate with individuals involved in close, personal sexual relationships, to increase the awareness and understanding of HIV and AIDS. In a phrase, HIV and AIDS touch and affect us all in some aspect or another.

Although the material covered in this text is applicable to all of us in some form or another, the voice of the book is geared to graduate students and upper-division undergraduates who are interested in interpersonal and health-related aspects of close relationships. The book is fitting for individuals interested in interpersonal, social, and health related issues working in a variety of disciplinary areas such as communication, sociology, psychology, social psychology, women's studies, and public health.

This book is structured to take the reader on a journey through a variety of close relationship types. To set the stage and tone of the book, chapter 1 brings to the reader's awareness the global enormity of HIV and AIDS and then provides a link between the global and the personal and the need to make HIV and AIDS part of our everyday talk and personal relational structure. The stage is set for script theory providing the developmental and guiding path throughout the text. Chapter 2 addresses safer sex in close, heterosexual dating relationships, focusing on the factors and communication involved in safer sex negotiation and practices. Chapter 3 brings the reader into marital relationships and the importance of safer sex discussion and awareness in marriage. Many consider the legal, social, and institutional nature of marriage to somehow make spouses immune to HIV. Lesser focus is given to spouses who might have entered the marriage being HIV positive or partners who engaged in risky practices (e.g., IV drug use or unprotected sex with a secondary partner) prior to or within the context of marriage. Chapter 4 focuses on safer sex in homosexual relationships and discusses the political, sociopolitical, and personal issues involved in such relationships. Championed in the chapter are how members of the homosexual community brought HIV and AIDS awareness to individuals' social consciousness, the change in sexual practices that resulted in the reduction of new infections among the homosexual community, and the need for younger homosexual males, in particular, to learn from those who preceded them in terms of their legacy of increased awareness and safer sex practices. Chapter 5 addresses HIV and AIDS from a multicultural perspective. Particular focus rests on identifying which messages resonate in what communities, descriptions of cultural variation, and prescriptions for success in increased awareness and safer sex practices. Chapter 6 focuses on HIV and AIDS in aged populations. Many do not perceive the elderly population as an at-risk population, unfortunately. With the onset of menopause and the resulting reduced risk for pregnancy, male-enhancement drug use, and increased dating practices of widows and widowers, many aged individuals are actively dating and engaging in sexual relationships. The purpose of this chapter is to increase awareness of the sexuality of this population and increasing aged individuals' awareness about a phenomenon that was nonexistent many years ago when many first entered the dating/courting aspect of their lives. Chapter 7 examines living with HIV and AIDS. The purpose of this chapter is to increase awareness, understanding, and compassion of those living with HIV and AIDS, and to explore their disclosure of their seropositive status, their personal relationships, and their engagement in close, intimate relationships of their own. Chapter 8 brings us to the conclusion of the book. Here, our attempt is to synthesize, bring the discussion full circle, and provide a rhetorical statement about just how quickly the face of HIV and AIDS is changing. Indeed, the number of HIV and AIDS cases (and, unfortunately, deaths due to AIDS) increased during the course of writing this text. In the conclusion, the main foci of each chapter are revisited and suggestions for future direction on these phenomena are proposed.

ACKNOWLEDGMENTS

Mike Allen wishes to acknowledge the continued support and confidence of Nancy Burrell and the assistance of many different people that have worked together on the research related to AIDS education and prevention, Katie Ksobiech, Mary K. Casey, Lisa Bradford, Erin Sahlstein, Kathleen Valde, Elizabeth Babin, and Lauren Hookham. Finally, a big thanks to Tara who originated the idea for this project and put up with my random work habits to complete this project.

Tara M. Emmers-Sommer wishes to acknowledge Tom, Evan, and Austin for their support and understanding of late nights. She also wishes to thank her family and friends, Alesia Hanzal, Perry Pauley, David Rhea, and Laura Triplett for their assistance with locating articles, Tara L. Crowell for her input on HIV/AIDS projects, Steve Duck for his support of this project and inclusion of it in his Personal Relationships Series with Lawrence Erlbaum Associates, the LEA team of Linda BAthgate, Karin Wittig-Bates, Paul Overmyer, and Sara Scudder as well as various others at LEA who assisted in bringing this project to fruition. Finally, many thanks go to Mike Allen for his efforts on this project, his friendship, and the opportunity to have done research with him for the past 15 years.

—*Tara M. Emmers-Sommer*
Mike Allen

Why Examine Safer Sex in Personal Relationships?

NATURE AND EXTENT OF THE PROBLEM

Approximately 2 decades after HIV and AIDS were originally discovered in 1981, 40 million individuals worldwide are living with HIV. Seventy percent of these individuals are Africans (World Health Organization [WHO], 2002). AIDS is the leading cause of death in Africa and the fourth leading cause of death universally (WHO, 2002). Within the United States, 774,467 individual cases of AIDS were reported to the Centers for Disease Control (CDC) between 1981 and 2000. Eighty-three percent of these cases involved men and 17% involved women. Of the 774,467 cases reported to the CDC, 448,060 of these individuals have perished (CDC, 2002). Until an effective vaccination program or curative treatment is developed, the numbers are expected to continue to increase. The worldwide implications of this growing problem are increasing as the Indian subcontinent (in late 2002 the estimate was over 4.5 million infected with an expectation of 25 million by the year 2010, *Milwaukee Journal*, 2002), the old Soviet Republics, and mainland China start to experience increases in infection. The full level of economic disruption and social dislocation from millions of AIDS orphans and loss of economic potential occurs. The evidence, particularly in Asia, is for a growing and impending crisis in the future that continues to intensify and become increasingly disruptive.

Over the past 2 decades, the media and much research have heavily focused on certain groups (e.g., gay and bisexual men, intravenous (IV) drug users, prostitutes) when examining HIV and AIDS. Indeed, at the onset of HIV and AIDS in the United States, the predominant groups afflicted by HIV and AIDS were men having sex with other men and intravenous drug users, particularly the former (CDC, 2002). Trends over the past 15 years, however, indicate a decrease in AIDS among men having sex with men and a plateauing of cases

1

among IV drug users. A marked increase in trend, however, exists for individuals diagnosed with AIDS due to heterosexual contact. In fact, in 2000, the individuals diagnosed with AIDS due to IV drug use and heterosexual contact were the same (i.e., 27%) (CDC, 2002).

Until 1985, the CDC had to rely on state reporting of AIDS cases for AIDS surveillance purposes. Due to the effectiveness of antiretroviral drug therapies for individuals afflicted with AIDS, the AIDS epidemic appeared to be quelling as AIDS trends no longer represented HIV incidence. As a result, it became necessary for states to instill confidential HIV case surveillance; thus, states reported AIDS and HIV cases, rather than only AIDS cases, to the CDC (CDC, 2002). The CDC cautioned that the confidential HIV surveillance incidence reportings are underestimates of the real rate of infection. Specifically, as of June 2001, approximately 14 states still did not participate in confidential HIV surveillance. Some of these 14 states include large populations and metropolitan areas (e.g., California, Maryland, Hawaii, Washington State, Illinois). Two states participated in pediatric HIV reporting only (Connecticut and Oregon) (CDC, 2002). Indeed, the scope of the problem is immense. A variety of pathways exist that enable a person to become HIV positive. The following section focuses on HIV transmission and its effects.

Transmission of HIV

Fluids. HIV can be transmitted in a number of manners. According to the CDC (2002), HIV can be passed through blood, semen, pre-seminal fluid, vaginal fluid, breast milk, or other bodily fluids containing blood. More specific to health care workers, the virus may also be passed via amniotic fluid supporting a fetus, synovial fluid around bone joints, and cerebrospinal fluid surrounding an individual's brain and spinal cord. The popular implication of this means of transmission is that HIV is not passed through "casual" contact or by someone just coughing or sneezing. HIV transmission requires contact with body fluids in a manner that permits entry into another person.

Modes of Entry. Information from the CDC indicates that HIV can enter the body through a number of areas including the anus, rectum, vagina, penis, mouth, veins (e.g., IV drug use), and other mucous membranes (CDC, 2002). This requirement for HIV transmission further reduces the expectation that casual contact will result in infection. The restricted means of entry makes HIV transmission usually linked to very identifiable and specific behaviors.

Behaviors Encouraging Transmission. Typically, HIV is transmitted by: (a) engaging in anal, oral, or vaginal sex with an HIV-infected individual, (b) sharing needles or other types of injection materials with an HIV-infected individual, and (c) HIV-infected mothers transmitting the virus to their baby before, during, or after birth (e.g., via breastfeeding). Although far less likely, HIV can be transmitted through contaminated blood transmitted via blood transfusions or needle-sticking, which is more specific to healthcare workers (CDC, 2002).

HIV's Transformation to AIDS. According to the CDC (2002), about half of the individuals who are infected with HIV will develop AIDS within a 10-year period. A variety of factors influence the effects of HIV in the body, including the individual's engagement in further risk behavior, engaging in preventative care, medical treatments, and so on. Clearly, HIV and AIDS awareness and education are important elements to individuals' understanding, communication, and behavioral modification. The following section addresses these issues within the context of managing HIV and AIDS in the future.

HIV AND AIDS: WHAT THE FUTURE HOLDS

According to the World Health Organization (2002), 15,000 individuals become infected with HIV daily and 95% of these cases are in developing countries. The World Health Organization contended that an AIDS vaccine is the most promising long-term solution to the HIV/AIDS epidemic, particularly in developing countries. As of yet, however, no vaccine exists, and the expectation for the development of a vaccine or curative treatment, although hopeful, does not appear immediate. Clearly, these data and information suggest that HIV and AIDS are of public concern. We contend that these data are also of personal and relational concern. Indeed, (lack of) communication about sexual activity involves both personal and relational implications. In a word, interpersonal communication is a health-related activity. That is, the nature of our communication affects our emotional, mental, and physical well-being. Currently, our strongest weapons against HIV infection involve knowledge, communication of that knowledge, and behavioral adherence to the safer sex practices espoused by the knowledge; that is, practicing interpersonal sexual scripts that encourage safer sex behaviors. The purpose of this book is to address safer sex issues in personal relationships. The following sections lay the definitional and theoretical groundwork. The theoretical framework offered in this chapter serves as a guide as the acquisition and evolution of scripts are discussed throughout the remainder of the text as they apply to a variety of personal relationship contexts. To begin, safer sex is defined.

DEFINITIONAL FRAMEWORK

We define *safer sex* as a description of any action a person takes to diminish the level of risk for HIV infection. Most frequently, the term is used to describe the use of a condom during sexual behavior to prevent contact with bodily fluids. However, there are a variety of practices that would be "safer" when compared to others. For example, instead of anal sex, a gay male couple could engage in sex using their hands (e.g., mutual masturbation). Performing oral sex, although believed to carry some risk, is "safer" than vaginal or anal sex. Modification or avoidance of some types of sexual acts would reduce the level of risk. Another method of reducing risk from sexual contact would be a reduction in the number of sexual partners (an exclusive mutually monogamous relationship between HIV-negative persons would carry virtually zero risk of infection). Avoiding persons with a history of intravenous drug use or a sexual history of unprotected and / or commercial sex reduces risk. These risk factors however require that the person ask or discuss with the potential partner as well as honestly disclose these facts about him- or herself. For many persons, discussion of the number of type of prior sexual acts with someone other than the current partner is generally considered inappropriate. This conversational topic, or the desire to have this conversation, for many persons would be considered a violation of the normal expectations about the script of sexual behavior between individuals. Many persons either do not want to hear and / or do not want to disclose this information to the other person. In fact, deception about the disclosure is not uncommon because of the fear that disclosure of information would diminish the possibility of sexual behavior with a partner (Lucchetti, 1998).

Overall, however, it is necessary to be mindful of the fact that none of these risk-reduction techniques are foolproof. Condoms break, fluids spill, sores bleed, and partners can lie or mislead about their personal practices. The only true "safe sex" is masturbation or abstinence. Given the low probability of that event taking place for a variety of social and personal reasons, the only recourse is some form of education and prevention that reduces the risk as much as possible for sexually active persons. The goal ought to involve the production and adoption of conversational strategies that become ingrained or accepted behavioral routines that involve safer sex. The goal of educational programs should be the installation of these routine patterns of behavior that are associated with safer sexual practices.

The primary theoretical framework guiding this project is script theory from a sexual, developmental perspective (Metts & Spitzberg, 1996; Simon & Gagnon, 1984, 1986, 1987). Specifically, we examine the sexual lifespan of individuals, beginning with adolescence and continued through later adulthood, and how the form and function of sexual scripts throughout the sexual lifespan are reshaped and renegotiated. This view of human interaction is associated with generalized approaches to communication that assume that humans develop scripts or schema (Mandler, 1984). The development of scripts is associated with theories relating to how persons develop a dynamic memory to handle and structure events and processes (Schank, 1982). The various manifestations of these approaches have become MOPs (memory organization packet, Kellermann, 1991), addressed through action assembly theory (Greene, 1984), or accounts (Schönbach, 1990). Each of these approaches examines the nature of how various interpersonal communication interactions are associated with the development of routines to handle the task. The work involves recognizing the situation and then employing the appropriate behavioral sequence to accomplish the appropriate communicative task in the situation.

Within this overarching set of theoretical frameworks are various approaches explaining human behavior that include some aspect of risk personalization (i.e., social learning theory, social exchange theory, personal motivation theory, social identity theory, uncertainty reduction theory, positive outcome value theory, expectancy violation theory, health belief model). This text incorporates recent research (e.g., Crowell & Emmers-Sommer, 2001) examining HIV positive individuals' attitudes, communication, and behaviors prior to and since their seropositivity, to establish sexual scripts in which safer sex discussions and practices are more conducive. A variety of communities exist that can be examined as they relate to the HIV / AIDS phenomenon. Some of these communities include lesbians, the mentally ill / retarded, the homeless, illegal aliens, minority populations, intravenous drug users, adolescents, commercial sex workers, gay males, and pregnant women. For the purposes of this book, the focus is personal relationships and how scripts are enacted and developed for individuals. However, a variety of sources of support exist that are available to various communities affected by HIV / AIDS. These sources of support include religious personnel, peers, family, and community leaders. Given that the focus of this text is on personal relationships, the following section addresses the nature of sexual scripts manifested in personal relationships.

SEXUAL SCRIPTS

Despite the statistics, most individuals still tend to perceive themselves as invulnerable to acquiring HIV or AIDS when compared to others (e.g., Raghubir & Menon, 1998). Within the context of close, personal relationships, the discussion and practice of safer sex is often perceived as unnecessary or as violating the expectations, assumptions, or script of the negotiated relationship (e.g., Crowell & Emmers-Sommer, 2001; Willing, 1994). Yet, it is at the close, interpersonal level between partners where such discussions and negotiations become most necessary. Sexual interaction remains something negotiated between individuals based on the notions of appropriateness brought into the situation (as well as the previous experience of both individuals with each other as well as previous encounters). Shimanoff (1980) points out that each participant brings to the encounter a set of rules or expectations about the nature of how any communication episode should take place. Each individual evaluates the behavior in the interaction and compares the conversation and actions to previous behavior. If a person acts inappropriately or strangely, the sexual encounter may be interrupted or terminated and each person unhappy with the outcome or consequences. Each person is under a bit of stress or tension to make the conversation fall within the expectations of the other person.

Thus, the purpose of this book is twofold. One purpose is to focus on safer sex discussion and practice in close, personal relationships. A second purpose is to focus on close, individuals in personal relationship types who are experiencing a rise in HIV infection and AIDS but are not receiving as much scholarly research attention as gay and bisexual adult males and IV drug-users. A goal of the book is to paint a clear picture of the very real risk that exists for these less-studied populations so that individuals may better personalize the risk and engage in more preventative measures. Specifically, research suggests that once individuals personalize the risk of HIV, there is an increased chance that they will change their attitude and engage in safer sexual behaviors (Ehde, Holm, & Robbins, 1995; Ishii-Kuntz, Whitbeck, & Simons, 1990; Raghubir & Menon, 1998; Timmins, Gallois, McCamish, & Terry, 1993). We propose to examine safer sex, primarily relying on research focusing on how individuals in the various aforementioned populations struggle with personalizing (or seek to avoid personalizing) the HIV and AIDS risk and how they cope with safer sex issues.

Individuals acquire sexual scripts in a variety of manners. For example, the role appropriateness of gender behavior is related to exposure to the media (Herrett-Skjellum & Allen, 1996). The search for role models and routines that are appropriate in a sexual encounter will reflect one particular source of information, the media. For many college students a major source of information about sexuality is pornography (Duncan, 1990; Duncan & Donnelly, 1991; Duncan & Nicholson, 1991), which typically does not include depictions of condom use. In addition, and as illustrated throughout the remainder of this book, individuals' sexual scripts evolve over the course of the lifespan. The role of sexual scripts in safer sexual behavior is a very salient one, as it affects safer sex practices (e.g., Hynie, Lydon, Coté, & Wiener, 1998; Maticka-Tyndale, 1991) and perceptions of susceptibility (Maticka-Tyndale, 1991). Sexual scripts have been described as cognitive structures that guide sexual behavior (Metts & Spitzberg, 1996) as well as stereotypical, expected, interactive behavior in social interactions (Abelson, 1981). In summary, sexual scripts serve as a mental roadmap, if you will, for how individuals are to conduct themselves in sexual situations. Sexual scripts are influenced at a number of levels, including cultural, interpersonal, and intrapsychic levels (Simon & Ganon, 1984, 1986, 1987). Interrelationships exist among the levels. Each of these three levels is examined further next.

Cultural Scripts

Cultural scripts are the most broad of the three levels of sexual scripts. Cultural scripts involve overall maps of sexual behavior at the societal level. In a word, cultural scripts address the "who, what, when, and where" aspects of sexual activity. Specifically, cultural scripts involve assessing who is appropriate to desire and pursue sexually, the accepted type of relationship between sexual partners, when and where partners should engage in sexual activity, and how partners are supposed to be feeling in regard to the sexual activity. These various structures contribute to how individuals are supposed to act and how they are supposed to interpret their experiences (Simon & Ganon, 1984, 1986, 1987). Cultural scripts provide a strong sense of social appropriateness or guidance about what "ought" to occur. One example of the impact of social scripts is the difficulty that homosexual parents have in obtaining custody of children and / or visitation rights. Despite clear empirical evidence summarized in a meta-analysis (Allen & Burrell, 1996, 2002), the fear of the violation of social scripts keeps biological parents that are gay away from their children.

Cultural scripts are largely influenced by the media (Metts & Spitzberg, 1996). This point is particularly salient to the context of this book, as young adolescents who are beginning to learn about sex and sexuality are likely to rely on media as a predominant source of information. A study conducted by Strasburger and Donnerstein (1999) found that children and adolescents relied heavily on television and other forms of media to learn about sexuality. In fact, as children enter adolescence, their primary source of information regarding sex, violence, and drugs changes. Specifically, a study conducted by the Kaiser Family foundation in conjunction with *Family Circle* magazine found that children aged 10 to 12 relied on mothers most often for information on sex, drugs, and violence. Children aged 13 to 15 relied on friends most for information on these topics and mothers as a source of information fell to fifth place. Overall, however, children between the ages of 10 to 15 relied on the media second most often for information regarding sex, drugs, and violence (Ebron, 1999). These findings suggest that children and adolescents rely heavily on media for sources of information on sex, drugs, and violence. In addition, consideration of a parent as a source of information diminishes as children enter adolescence and reliance on peers for information increases (Mazur, 2001). This finding is of potential concern as peers might be misinformed about sex, drug, or violence issues and the media's representation of these issues is not necessarily realistic or accurate. The type and tone of the media information gleaned by young adolescents greatly varies, from realistic, educational fare to violent or fantasized images portrayed through pornography. For example, Brown and Bryant (1989) found that the majority of females and males had seen or read *Playgirl* or *Playboy* by the age of 15. Allen, Emmers, Gebhardt, and Giery (1995) found that some media images portrayed through pornography suggest the acceptability of violence and coercion (e.g., rape) in an effort to gain sex. Portrayals of traditionalism and male dominance can affect men's and women's ideologies and scripts about what they are supposed to do in sexual situations versus what they might want to do (e.g., Byers, 1996; Emmers-Sommer, 2002; Emmers-Sommer & Allen, 1999). Other media images (e.g., television shows, movies) rarely include a discussion or use of condoms prior to engaging in sexual activity. This is concerning given that many adolescents coming into puberty receive information about sexual behavior from sources that involve misrepresentation, inaccuracies, or glorification of violence. In that context, the script for sexual behavior will not involve a consideration of the other person or of the need for safer sexual behaviors as a means of disease protection.

Intrapsychic Scripts

Intrapsychic scripts involve "individual desires, motives, and actions that create and sustain sexual arousal" (Metts & Spitzberg, 1996, p. 52). Hynie et al. (1998) argued that "intrapsychic scripts are the internalization of the socially shared scripts and scenarios. Social competence requires social performance of cultural scenarios which, in turn, requires rehearsal of interpersonal scripts based on those scenarios" (p. 2). Hynie et al. (1998) also argued that the internalization of intrapsychic scripts plays a role in how interpersonal scripts are carried out. Such scripts reflect individual desires as well as expectations about social interaction. Evidence from convicted sexual offenders illustrates how the level of sexual arousal is related to the desires of the individual for particular sexual acts (Allen, D'Alessio, & Emmers-Sommer, 1999). Sexuality can function to fulfill individual needs for relationships, power, physical gratification, procreation, etc. If one views sexuality as an enactment of a behavior to fulfill individual needs, the extent to which a person views a sexual interaction as fulfilling will be related to how the particular action instantiates the unique expectations for how a satisfying sexual encounter proceeds. The generation of the individual script or sequence of behavior for the satisfying encounter reflects a combination of individual, cultural, and social influence that have combined to generate in the mind of the individual the requirements and expectations for script for sexual actions. A critical aspect of educational and therapeutic interventions requires that expectations change to modify sexual scripts toward safer and/or less abusive sequences that will lead to satisfaction from more socially acceptable patterns of behavior.

Interpersonal Scripts

Individuals' own personal experiences and histories affect their interpersonal scripts (Hynie et al., 1998). Specifically, interpersonal scripts are formed by an individual's interpretation of the cultural script and their internalization of their intrapsychic scripts (Hynie et al., 1998; Metts & Spitzberg, 1996). Hynie et al. argued, "In other words, rehearsal of interpersonal scripts derived from cultural scenarios actually shapes individual attitudes, values and beliefs and, in this manner, interpersonal scripts act as the link between individual attitudes and societal norms" (p. 2). Sexual scripts reflect the need to create regular and recognizable patterns of behavior so that all parties in the sexual act know what actions are expected or required. Sexual practices become events that are negotiated between or among individual persons and each participant needs to recognize the role played in the script. Actions that fall outside of the script come as a surprise and make a person vulnerable by potentially betraying an ignorance or lack of experience about expected behavior, a label of deviance or perversion, the potential to disappoint the partner, or frustration from a partner unable or unwilling to perform the sequence that would give the person sexual satisfaction. Such uncertainty and anxiety about sexual scripts creates the pressure to avoid actions that could possibly be interpreted negatively by a partner.

Although adherence to and evaluation of sexual scripts are helpful in understanding what contributes to guidance of sexual behavior, sexual scripts do not explain all of the variance in our sexual behavior. Indeed, other factors exist that contribute to our attitudes about sexuality and sexual behavior. The following section examines other predominant factors that influence sexual attitudes and behaviors. These factors include self-efficacy as it relates to negotiation of condom use, perceptions of invulnerability, trust, and perceptions of a safe partner. Although certainly not exhaustive, these factors have nevertheless demonstrated influence on individuals' safer sex attitudes and behaviors in much of the safer sex research.

FACTORS AFFECTING SAFER SEX BEHAVIOR

Self-efficacy

Within the context of safer sex practices, Hynie et al. (1998) argued that individuals' interpersonal scripts might explain why individuals' attitudes and their awareness of social norms can fail to predict individuals' behavior in sexual situations. Specifically, the authors argued that knowledge of the appropriate script in a given situation is related to how an individual performs in a given situation. Thus, a when a discrepancy exists between the adherence to certain behaviors and knowledge on how to put those behaviors into action, individuals are less inclined to behave in a manner aligned with their attitudes. This notion is tied to an individual's self-efficacy in regard to safer sex practices (e.g., Bandura, 1977). Self-efficacy should not be confused with response efficacy. Self-efficacy addresses the issues of the individual to feel empowered to implement the script necessary to increase safer sexual practices, whereas response efficacy is the expectation that a person has that the practice will in fact be safer and reduce the probability of contracting HIV. A central element of self-efficacy is the consideration of what motivates a person to feel confident and comfortable enacting a sexual script that increases the probability of safer sexual practices.

Crowell and Emmers-Sommer (2000), however, examined condom use self-efficacy and coping in sexual situations and found that high condom efficacy was weakly correlated with actual condom use. Participants also relied more on noncommunicative ways of coping (e.g., avoidance) in sexual situations than communicative ways of coping. Individuals' always using a condom for sex was related to communicative ways of coping. Efficacy was positively related to communicative coping styles. Hynie et al. (1998), in a series of three studies, examined the relationship between scripted sociosexual norms on women's contraceptive behavior. Study one involved men's and women's evaluations initial sexual encounter scripts. Results found that women portrayed the female character as more relational than the male character. Study two gathered information on relational ideals from female participants. Study three used women's relational ideal from study two to predict women's contraceptive attitudes and behavior. Results indicated that when sexual attitudes were controlled, adherence to the relational ideal related to less positive attitudes toward condoms, a reduced likelihood of condom use during their previous intercourse, and less likelihood to obtain contraceptives in relationships. Hynie et al.'s findings are similar to other works that found support for a greater likelihood that women embrace the relational ideal in terms of sexuality whereas men focus more on the self and pleasure (e.g., Byers, 1996; DeLamater, 1987).

Perceived Invulnerability

Research indicates that if individuals are not willing to personalize the risk of HIV, they are not likely to engage in safer sex behaviors (e.g., Crowell & Emmers-Sommer, 2001). Unfortunately, many infected individuals are not aware of their seropositivity and might be passing the virus unknowingly (Sternberg, 2002). Indeed, many individuals perceive themselves to be invulnerable to acquiring HIV (e.g., Ehde, Holm, & Robbins, 1995). According to Sternberg (2002), the CDC reports that more than 75% of gay and bisexual men who are infected with HIV do not know it and the individuals involved in a CDC study who did test positive had perceived themselves to be low risk. In addition to gay and bisexual men, many heterosexuals perceive themselves to be low risk in terms of acquiring HIV and, as a result, do not engage in safer sex practices (e.g., Cantania, Coates, Stall, & Turner, 1992). Thus, it is necessary to understand what psychological and social psychological components contribute to an individual's decision to acquire or not acquire safer sex behaviors (Wulfert & Wan, 1995). In a word, it is necessary to understand what contributes to an individual adopting safer sex behaviors as part of their sexual script.

Trust

Another construct that affects individuals' sexual behavior in personal relationships is the degree of trust that they have for their partner. Research indicates that individuals who believe that they are in monogamous relationships and have high trust for their partner often do not use condoms during sexual encounters (e.g., Crowell & Emmers-Sommer, 2000; Ishii-Kuntz et al., 1990; Pilkington, Kern, & Indest, 1994). As relationships become more exclusive, partners tend to forego condoms in favor of other forms of birth control (e.g., the pill) (Metts & Fitzpatrick, 1992). Indeed the research indicates that heterosexual couples often associate condom use with birth control versus a barrier to sexually transmitted diseases (e.g., Maticka-Tyndale, 1991; Lear, 1995; Sonnex, Hart, Williams, & Adler, 1989). An examination of safer sex in marital relationships found that 96% of the married partners associated condoms with birth control instead of safer sex (see Chapter 3). After all, if a person is married, the assumption of monogamy made by most couples becomes part of the definition of the relationship and the need for safer sex behaviors should not exist. The definition of the relationship makes the discussion of safer sex behaviors simply unnecessary and the introduction of such discussion becomes associated with accusations of relational violation.

Perceptions of trust and commitment in personal relationships negatively relates to engagement in safer sex behaviors. Unfortunately, many individuals who perceive themselves to be low risk are in error (Crowell & Emmers-Sommer, 2001; Sternberg, 2002). A study conducted by Cochran and Mays (1990) found that both men and women engaged in deception in an effort to gain sex from their partner. Crowell and Emmers-Sommer (2001) examined seropositive individuals' attitudes and behaviors prior to infection. Individuals reported moderately high trust in their relationships and perceptions of partner safety. Together, these variables explained over 40% of the variance in perceived risk of HIV infection. Many of the individuals in the authors' sample were infected by serious relational or marital partners. Collectively, these data suggest that individuals in close, personal relationships still need to be cognizant of the fact that they are not invulnerable to HIV or STDs. Given the 40 to 60% infidelity rate indicated by some studies (Emling, 2000), it is necessary for partners to include discussion of sexual practices in their relationships and make it an acceptable part of one's sexual script.

Safe Partner

As just mentioned, perceptions of partner safety relate to a reduction in safer sex behavior. Crowell and Emmers-Sommer (2000) found that perceptions of a monogamous relationship, relationship length, and seriousness of the relationship contributed to individuals' perceptions that their partner was "safe." Similarly, Metts and Fitzpatrick argued that many individuals believe that they do not need to use condoms to engage in safer sex because they are already choosing a partner who is "safe" (1992). Unfortunately, many individuals erroneously believe that they can distinguish a "safe" partner from an "unsafe" partner (Ishii-Kuntz et al., 1990). Research indicates that many individuals believe that partners who hail from their own social network are "safe" because they are similar to themselves (e.g., Ishii-Kuntz et al., 1990; Timmons, Gallois, McCamish, & Terry, 1996). Specifically, individuals often grasp onto the notion of "I am fine and I would not associate with you if you were not fine, too." Once again the acceptance of beliefs about the nature of the other person that are assumed makes the development of safer sex script difficult because the script that would lead to the use of condom requires a fundamental alteration of the view of the other person. Rather than presuming that the other person is safe or has similar values, it is important for partners to be open and communicate about their feelings and behaviors. Such practices are important at all stages of relationships, from adolescence through sexual relationships of the aged. Indeed, safer sex is not a concern solely for middle-aged homosexual and bisexual men. HIV knows no boundaries due to age, sex, or sexual practice. Thus, it is important to examine safer sex in a variety of relational contexts. The problem is that the mere introduction of the topic and the questions or request for behavior carries implications in current social relationships.

Even for gay males where the knowledge level and openness and acceptability of a condom request is far higher than heterosexual the communities, the request to wear a condom carries with it the risk of not having a sexual encounter, even in an environment as sexually open as a bathhouse (Elwood & Williams, 1999). As one of the participants in the Elwood and Williams (1999) study said, "I just had to have him, you know? I thought about using condoms, I did, but I didn't want to talk because it might break the moment, or he might go away. I just had to have him, so I backed onto him.... I knew what the risks were, but I didn't care" (p. 127). Even when the generally accepted or social preferred script is known and available, the issues of sexual gratification and the fear of social or relational embarrassment reduce the level of safer sex behaviors.

PREVIEW OF CHAPTERS

As noted, this text approaches safer sex in personal relationships from a sexual script theory approach. More specifically, an emphasis is placed on how scripts develop and evolve in a variety of relationship contexts as well as their developmental paths over the course of a sexual lifespan. Next, specifics of the remaining chapters in this text are previewed.

Chapter 2: Safer Sex in Heterosexual Dating Relationships. Unlike the practices of many adult gay and bisexual males, safer sex discussion and practice (e.g., condom use) are not part of the heterosexual romantic culture or script. Many establishments where heterosexuals gather and socialize are not peppered with HIV / AIDS public service announcements. Condom machines are hidden away in the bathrooms and payment is necessary to access a condom. This chapter examines the (lack of) safer sex discussion and practice in heterosexual young adult and adult sexual relationships. The struggle many couples experience between being involved in a trusting, close personal relationship and the discussion of safer sex, sexual histories, and risky behavior (e.g., infidelity) is explored as well as how adolescents and adults can work such discussions into their sexual scripts.

Chapter 3: Safer Sex in Marriage. Issues that exist in Chapter 2 are compounded in Chapter 3. Sexual scripts in marital relationships are examined as well as the implications of societal, religious, and institutional expectations on such relationships. Specifically, issues of trust, intimacy, commitment, religious and institutional recognition of the relation- ship, and the like are examined as they relate to safer sexual behavior in a marital relationship and how such constructs are affected by behaviors of unfaithfulness and infidelity. Issues that are commonly perceived as dating, but not marital, concerns are explored and how such issues are woven into marital sexual scripts.

Chapter 4: Homosexual Relationships and Safer Sex.   This chapter primarily focuses on young gay males. Much of the research suggests that many adult gay males have personalized the AIDS risk and engage in safer sexual behavior because many experienced the AIDS epidemic of the 1980s firsthand. Many adult gay males experienced the loss of an acquaintance, friend, or loved one and were thus able to identify and personalize the risk of HIV. Gay bars often have bowls of condoms on the bar as opposed to peanuts, public service announcement posters are prevalent, and discussion of safer sex and condom use is part of the culture. Research indicates, however, a return to risky behavior for many young, gay males. Reasons for a return to risky behavior are largely due to new drug therapies and treatments (e.g., AIDS drug cocktails). As a result, more young gay males are taking part in "barebacking," which involves anonymous, unprotected sex, where discussions of HIV status and condom use are forbidden.

Chapter 5: Culture and Safer Sex Behaviors.   This chapter focuses primarily on HIV and condom use in Hispanic, Native American, Asian American, and African American cultures and personal relationships. Cultural issues such as machismo, traditionalism, religion, and reliance on families for information versus the media or educational system are explored. Similar to other populations addressed in this text, young adults' and adolescents' perceptions of invulnerability are explored. Finally, this chapter focuses on how these cultural issues manifest themselves into close, personal relationships and how they affect sexual scripts.

Chapter 6: Safer Sex and the Aged.   One very understudied population regarding safer sex is the elderly. Many individuals erroneously associate HIV and AIDS as something afflicting the young. However, research indicates that aged adults often have sex sooner in their relationship than young individuals and typically do not discuss modes of birth control (e.g., condoms) because it is not perceived as necessary. Yet, research indicates that over 60,000 adults over the age of 50 have been diagnosed with HIV or AIDS. As individuals live longer and more drug therapies are at their disposal to aid in sex lives (e.g., Viagra), discussion of safer sex is necessary. Thus, this chapter focuses on the need for such discussions, the prevalence of such discussions, and suggestions on how the aged might integrate such discussions into their sexual scripts.

Chapter 7: Safer Sex and Living With HIV/AIDS. Societal language in the United States regarding HIV and AIDS has changed somewhat since the 1980s. Specifically, with the influx of more successful drug treatments and therapies, many individuals are "living" with AIDS as opposed to "dying" of AIDS. Research suggests that many individuals who are HIV positive or who are in various stages of AIDS experience close, personal relationships and manage to maintain those relationships during the illness. Safer sex is still an issue with seropositive individuals because: (a) their partner may be HIV negative, or (b) the risk of reinfection exists for seropositive individuals. That is, their drug therapy is designed to fight their personal strain of HIV, but is not able to fight off another strain of HIV that could be acquired through unprotected sex. This chapter focuses on how individuals living with HIV and AIDS reshape and renegotiate their sexual scripts within their close, personal relationships.

Chapter 8: Conclusion. The final chapter offers several conclusions suggested by the previous chapters. First, the consistencies across relationships are highlighted. Second, inconsistencies across relationship-type are addressed (i.e., scripts and behaviors particular to a certain relationship-type). Specifically, the developmental path of sexual scripts are synthesized and discussed. Third, the implications for sexual script acquisition, reshaping, and renegotiating are discussed. Finally, the strengths and weaknesses of the extant research are assessed and discussed.

The essential case being made is to find method of incorporating AIDS education and prevention information as a part of the formation and enactment of social scripts for various activities. Making the use of prevention behaviors that reduce the spread of the disease reduces the practices from conscious to unconscious routinized behavior. The development of these scripts and the placement of the behavioral routines in memory represents the ultimate goal of safer sex education. Overcoming the resistance and apprehension associated with sexual behavior, and the silences associated with sexual practice, represent fundamental barriers that require the attention of the communication scientists if such programs are to be effective.

Safer Sex in Heterosexual Dating Relationships

The advent of AIDS was initially treated as a disease that affected persons outside the norm of the heterosexual majority (homosexuals, bisexuals, commercial sex workers, and intravenous drug users). The result of this perception was a difficult period of denial where heterosexuals could essentially ignore the warning messages that were issued about the disease because the virus was determined to affect a different set of populations. After all, any condition or disease believe to impact on the "other" is something that the majority does not have to worry about. The acceptance of this infectious virus as something impacting some other group of people permits an audience to ignore or misinterpret messages. Despite years of trying to lessen the stigma associated with HIV / AIDS and the mythologies, evidence demonstrates difficulty in changing fundamental views (Brown, Macintyre, & Trujillo, 2003).

This lack of concern, because the early population affected by HIV was not heterosexual, can be viewed as a mistake when examining the spread of the disease in Africa. The overwhelming majority of cases in Africa are the result of unprotected heterosexual behavior. The perception of the disease in the United States remains that largely of something associated with white gay males (promiscuous and anal sex practitioners) or intravenous drug users. This perception creates a sense of deniability for the heterosexual in the United States when considering or evaluating the risk.

The first major celebrity (viewed as heterosexual) to contract HIV was Earvin "Magic" Johnson. His announcement created a media sensation that did generate some significant changes in the level of knowledge and behavior in the United States (for a summary of the research see Casey et al., 2003). The most significant effect based on age was the adults' report that Johnson's announcement made them more knowledgeable about the transmission of HIV and increased their level of anxiety about AIDS. This finding is not surprising when one considers that

Magic Johnson contracting the virus represents a very public affirmation that the virus does not only infect gay males and drug users. A famous heterosexual athlete contracting the virus made the virus something directly applicable to the heterosexual community. The infection of "Magic" Johnson indicated the celebrity and excellent physical health did not bar a person from getting the virus. Of course, a person could view the celebrity as different from themselves and still not find anything of value to correspond to their own lives (rumors circulated that Earvin Johnson was gay after the announcement).

The review (Casey et al., 2003) goes on to demonstrate that children's level of knowledge about HIV and AIDS increased (even more than adults), but that anxiety about the disease diminished. This finding probably indicates that children, by increasing knowledge about virus transmission, became less anxious because they were not at risk for infection. The virus became associated with "adult" behavior that third graders were not likely to engage in. More importantly, the messages associated with the announcement functioned to reassure children that hugging and simple human contact would not spread the virus. The increase in accurate knowledge about the method of transmission for the virus represents something that allays the fear of the third graders. However, the heterosexual adults demonstrate significant **increases** in anxiety. Improved and accurate information illustrates and corrects the errors in the perception of risk. More importantly, the threat of the disease increases in relevance to the listener and becomes less likely to be denied.

Despite the relatively high level of knowledge among the population in the United States about HIV transmission (e.g., Bruce, Shrum, Trefethen, & Slovik, 1990), the impact has not fundamentally affected safer sex practices among heterosexuals (e.g., condom use). Condom use is still primarily viewed as a means of birth control rather than disease prevention (e.g., Metts & Fitzpatrick, 1992). The purpose of this chapter is to further examine the abandonment of safer sex messages and practices by much of the heterosexual community. To do so, several theoretical perspectives are reviewed. Second, heterosexual dating relationships are compared to marital relationships in terms of factors affecting safer sex discussion and practice in close heterosexual, dating relationships and the implications of dating relationships being more tenuous or fleeting. Third, gender issues as they relate to sexual practices in heterosexual dating relationships are examined, with particular focus on women in such relationships. Finally, implications and suggestions for future directions are offered.

SAFER SEX DISCUSSION

As indicated earlier, seroprevalence in adult homosexual relationships is tapering off, but appears to be on the rise in heterosexual relationships. A variety of reasons exist for this seeming trend. First, despite warnings by the CDC, many heterosexuals do not perceive HIV and AIDS to be a heterosexual issue. That is, many heterosexuals perceive HIV and AIDS to be a homosexual phenomenon. Thus, communicating about sexual histories, IV drug use, safer sex practices, or even engaging in safer sex practices are perceived as unnecessary by numerous heterosexuals. Related, individuals who do discuss STDs, HIV, and necessary safer sex practices often receive mixed reception to their voiced concerns. Specifically, some individuals perceive such discussions as socially and personally responsible. Others, however, perceive such individuals as "taboo" in some way, as if the individual is engaging in such discussion because he or she is personally infected. Added, some individuals take offense to the mention of discussion of safer sex histories or the engagement in safer sex practices in the sense that they feel as though their own personal choices, practices or serostatus are being called into question. Indeed, Baxter and Wilmot (1985) found that discussion of sexual issues is often perceived as "taboo topics" during relationship development. Allen, Emmers-Sommer, and Crowell (2002) found that several factors need to be taken into consideration when considering safer sex discussion in heterosexual relationships. These factors include timing (i.e., mentioning the topics too soon might scare a partner off), social norms (i.e., not "kissing and telling"), personal privacy, and the awkwardness associated with such discussions.

Indeed, discussion of sexual histories, IV drug use, and safer sex practices are often perceived as a delicate situation. Yet, engagement in such discussion is imperative in dating relationships. Unlike marital relationships, which experience several barriers to dissolution (Attridge, 1994), dating relationships are not bound by the ties and commitments—legal or otherwise—that marital relationships experience. In a word, it is typically easier to be deceptive or exit the relationship quickly in dating contexts. Urban legend or not, many have heard horror stories about individuals engaging in sex while on vacation, or spring break, or with dating partners only to learn later—after the partner is out of sight or out of town—that he or she had an STD or HIV. Because few barriers to dissolution exist in dating unions, individuals in heterosexual dating relationships need to take precautions to protect themselves and their partner.

THEORETICAL PERSPECTIVES

As mentioned earlier, many individuals perceive HIV and AIDS to be a homosexual phenomenon. A variety of theoretical perspectives exist that explain how such beliefs are perpetuated and reinforced. Two particularly relevant theoretical perspectives are social identity theory (Tajfel & Turner, 1979) and social comparison theory (Festinger, 1954). Both theories are reviewed next, with particular focus on their saliency in the context of safer sex issues. Similarly, from a communication standpoint, one can draw conclusions about how one's sexual script is affected and practiced in the public and personal sphere based on one's ingroup and outgroup beliefs.

Social Identity Theory

Social identity theory (Tajfel & Turner, 1979), for example, argues self-concept involving personal and social identity characteristics from an intergroup perspective. Personal identity involves one's own unique aspects, personal attributes, likes and dislikes. Social identity involves how individuals identify themselves as members of a particular social group. This theoretical perspective is particularly salient to issues of HIV and AIDS because HIV and AIDS have been perceived by many heterosexuals as an outgroup phenomena (i.e., issues specific to homosexual groups). Individuals try to create unique identities for their group and their group membership and also try to distinguish themselves from outgroups and outgroup members. If discussion of HIV and AIDS as well as safer sex practices are deemed as outgroup discussions and relevant to homosexuals, then many heterosexuals will avoid such discussions and practices. In fact, such avoidance might be consciously purposeful in an attempt to reinforce ingroup status and identification.

The same argument can be made for individuals resigning from discussing intravenous (IV) drug use or men who have had bisexual experiences. Specifically, many individuals who have dabbled in IV drug use do not perceive themselves to be IV drug users. That is, such individuals distinguish recreational use from habitual users. The same identification often occurs with smokers, who describe themselves as nonsmokers, but who sometimes smoke socially. Many individuals who have engaged in recreational IV drug use will not reveal such practices, given that they are stigmatized practices, to potential sexual partners. Indeed, many might rationalize the past behavior as, "I only tried injecting a few times, but I am not a junkie" and thus, perceive that there is no need to share such information with partners. Unfortunately, however, it only takes one injecting episode to become infected with HIV or other STDs (e.g., hepatitis) if the needle used is infected. Similarly, many men who have engaged in sex with other men do not categorize themselves as homosexual or bisexual. Rather, such episodes are often chalked up as something they "tried" or "did" when they were under the influence of alcohol or drugs or did out of curiosity. Again, many such men do not believe that there is a need to share this information with a potential female partner as an attempt to reinforce their heterosexual ingroup status and mobilize themselves away from the homosexual or bisexual camps. Indeed, social identity theory can explain a heterosexual's lack of safer sex discussion, practices, and the refraining of discussion of certain sexual or drug-related practices in one's past.

Social Comparison Theory

Another related and relevant theoretical perspective is social comparison theory. Social comparison theory (Festinger, 1954) argues that individuals judge their own personal characteristics and situations by comparing themselves to others in a variety of areas, including health-related situations such as health risk (Klein & Weinstein, 1998), coping (Wood, Taylor, & Lichtman, 1985), behavior cessation (Gibson, Gerrard, Lando, & McGovern, 1991), and illness symptoms (Sanders, 1982). Social comparison theory might be particularly relevant to the HIV and AIDS contexts because such contexts are certainly threatening to one's well being. Tigges, Wills, and Link (1998) found that social comparison behaviors might differ between threatening versus nonthreatening situations. Specifically, when threatened, individuals often engage in downward comparisons (Wills, 1981). Downward comparisons involve comparing oneself to others who are perceived as different or worse off. Research suggests that individuals make such downward comparisons in health related contexts (e.g., Tigges et al., 1998). "Downward comparisons with regard to HIV could be one explanation for why individuals evaluate their risk of infection as little to none" (Crowell & Emmers-Sommer, 2001, p. 304). In an experiment, Rye (1998) found that when seronegative individuals were exposed to individuals perceived as similar to them, but who were also HIV positive, that the individuals' perceptions of vulnerability rose as did their intentions to discuss safer sex in the future and use a condom. Thus, enabling individuals to become more acquainted with individuals with HIV and AIDS is one way of lessening the gap between the groups that exist in the minds of many seronegative individuals. Crowell and Emmers-Sommer (2001) argued, from a social comparison theory perspective, that an individual's perception of invulnerability needed to be replaced with an individual's perception of risk.

The problem is that the method of transmission of the virus involves usually a violation of some social rule. The person with HIV can be considered "stupid" because that person engaged in indiscriminate sex, used drugs, or practiced some perversion (homosexuality). The sense of moral superiority permits the discounting of any risk that the person does engage in. Social comparison permits the person to develop en emotional position that carries a sense of invulnerability and lack of susceptibility to risk. The problem with practicing safer sexual behaviors is that it requires the omission by the individual that they are in fact like everyone else and vulnerable. Factors that influence perceptions of invulnerability and lack of condom use among heterosexual individuals are reviewed below.

FACTORS AFFECTING CONDOM USE
IN HETEROSEXUAL RELATIONSHIPS

A variety of factors affecting a heterosexual individuals' perceived invulnerability have already been reviewed (e.g., not being a habitual drug user, not characterizing oneself as homosexual or bisexual). Other factors exist, more specific to the context of heterosexual dating relationships and are elaborated on next.

Effect of Antiviral Therapies on Heterosexuals

The primary appeal used in public health campaigns to generate increased condom use is some form of the fear appeal. Essentially, the fear appeal provides for dire consequences for failure to comply with the behavior outlined in the message. The perception of a person dying from AIDS Related Condition (ARC) is a death from some type of terrible cancer, pneumonia, or some other disease. The image of persons dying from AIDS resembles that of persons shrunken, diseased, weak, ugly, and in great pain. The image of the disease is one that inspires fear. The serious consideration of AIDS patients committing suicide rather than die from the infections represents a particularly undesirable image (Copeland, 1993; Glass, 1988; Mancoske, Wadsworth, Dugas, & Haney, 1995; Schneider, Taylor, Hammen, Kemeny, & Dudley, 1991). However, advances in treatment of HIV and opportunistic infections mean that HIV infected persons can expect both a longer life and a higher quality life. However, as each advance is made in the treatment of HIV and the ability to treat AIDS grows, there is a corresponding reduction in the fear of the disease. Effective treatment reduces the disease from one that is immediately life threatening to one that represents a serious chronic condition (at least for those with access to therapy). One of the authors has interviewed persons practicing unsafe sexual practices and believe that if they do become infected they will simply take drugs.

Recent research (Allen et al., 2002; Catz, Meredith, & Mundy, 2001; Gagnon & Godin, 2000) indicates that the recent development of increasingly effective treatments for HIV infection continue to lower the fear of HIV/AIDS. The reduction in fear becomes associated with a decline in the motivation to use safer sex techniques as well as diminishing the number of sexual partners. Essentially, the increase in the effectiveness of therapies diminishes the impact of education and prevention efforts by undermining the perception of the severity of the threat, an important element of successful fear appeal messages related to health (Witte & Allen, 2000).

The impact of improved treatment and commercials that advertise that treatment will further erode the effectiveness of AIDS education and prevention efforts. For a population (heterosexual) that has already refused to identify with the disease (making the disease something associated with homosexuality or intravenous drug use), any decline in motivational efforts carries potentially serious consequences. Simply put, as the perception that HIV is not dangerous increases, the motivation to practice safer sexual procedures diminishes.

Perceptions of "Safe" Partner

Related to the theoretical perspectives mentioned earlier, many individuals perceive themselves as only engaging in sex with a "safe" partner and that infected individuals are somehow distinguishable from uninfected individuals (Timmins et al., 1993). Specifically, individuals rationalize, "I am safe and I would only have sex with other individuals who are safe." Such rationalization aligns with mobilizing with ingroup members or engaging in comparisons with similar others. Parallel to this line of reasoning, many individuals believe that they do not need to use condoms because the partner they choose to have sex with is "safe" (Metts & Fitzpatrick, 1992). Related, (Ishii-Kuntz et al., 1990) found that among college students, condom use was perceived as unnecessary because individuals chose partners from their own social network who were thus, perceived as safe. In a study of seropositive individuals, Crowell and Emmers-Sommer (2001) found that women were significantly more likely than men to have perceived their partner as "safe" before they became HIV positive. This is concerning, and health implications for women will be further examined later in this chapter.

Perceptions of Monogamy

Related to the contention just discussed of safe partner is the perception of monogamy in heterosexual dating relationships. Specifically, many heterosexuals perceive "sleeping around" and "promiscuity" to be practices more germane to homosexual or bisexual relationships. Although perhaps monogamy is part of a socialized ideology, many individuals do not ascribe to such beliefs or practices. Numerous studies indicate moderate to high levels of cheating in heterosexual relationships (e.g., Emling, 2000; Stebleton & Rothenberger, 1993). Other research has found a lack of partners' discussion of sexual histories (Stebleton & Rothenberger, 1993) or the outright use of lying and deception to gain sex from a potential partner (Cochran & Mays, 1990). These practices also exist among individuals who were knowingly seropositive (CNN News, 1998). Nevertheless, perceptions of monogamy and dating one partner versus multiple partners relates to reduced likelihood of using condoms. The problem is that asking the question represents a fundamental face threat for both individuals involving an assumption that the honesty of the other is in question. Also, the person asking the questions is admitting the inability to judge the character of a potential sexual partner.

With marital relationships comes an increased level of perceived commitment (Knapp & Taylor, 1994). Often, combined financial resources, familial networks, children, religious, legal, and institutional obligations can affect a person's ability to readily leave a relationship (Attridge, 1994). Although we certainly do not contend that an individual cannot be unfaithful to his or her spouse, we argue that conditions exist that make leaving the relationship quickly difficult. Thus, spouses might experience a greater likelihood of having opportunities to talk or actually having to talk given that more is at stake if sexual indiscretions occur. In a dating relationship, one could literally cut ties immediately with little to no obligation to the partner. The research is clear that many dating relationships are tenuous and fleeting (e.g., Berscheid, Snyder, & Omoto, 1989).

Length of Relationship

Length and seriousness of the relationship is related to condom use (Crowell & Emmers-Sommer, 2000). Specifically, individuals who have been involved in a relationship for a long period of time or who believe that the relationship is serious or exclusive are less likely to use condoms or engage in safer sex discussions (Crowell & Emmers-Sommer, 2001). Furthermore, and related to partner trust, individuals in longstanding relationships are more likely to change their choices in birth control measures. Specifically, individuals might use condoms early on in the relationship, before the relationship is well-established. However, partners' birth control choices are more likely to evolve as the relationship progresses (e.g., Lear, 1995; Metts & Fitzpatrick, 1992). Among heterosexual couples, condoms are often perceived as birth control devices rather than as useful in the prevention of STDS and HIV (e.g., Maticka-Tyndale, 1991). The assumption made by members engaged in a relationship is that the longer the relationship, the more exclusive and the greater the level of commitment. Religions and public officials have stated that the safest sexual practice is to be in a committed and exclusive relationship. Essentially, the assumption that monogamy is safe provides now a kind of test for the relationship. The test is that the lack of a condom becomes a marker, which can be used by the individuals, of the existence of a committed and exclusive relationship. The idea that lack of a condom indicates the evolution of a relationship from an unsafe to a safe stage permits relaxation and greater emotional satisfaction. The problem is that given a population with a great deal of infidelity and misrepresentation as well and uncertain guidelines about when this step is achieved creates the potential for additional risk over the longer term. As indicated in chapter 3, the same perception exists among married couples.

Partner Trust

Related to some of the previously mentioned concepts, partner trust has been found to reduce one's perception of vulnerability in terms of HIV and AIDS and also reduces likelihood of engaging in safer sex practices. Specifically, individuals who report high trust, liking, love, and/or commitment for their partner are less likely to use condoms (e.g., Crowell & Emmers-Sommer, 2000; Pilkington et al., 1994). Other research has also found that condom use tends to be abandoned when relational commitment and trust are achieved (Metts & Fitzpatrick, 1992). Crowell and Emmers-Sommer (2001) found that partner trust, in addition to perceptions of partner safety, explained 40% of the variance in perceptions of perceived risk among individuals before they became seropositive. Although these aforementioned factors affect both heterosexual men's and women's decisions and practices in relationships, the implications might be more concerning for women compared to men.

What happens is that when HIV infection occurs, there is a sense of relational betrayal. The person was trusting that the other member was reflecting the same values and behaviors (assuming that one of the two persons was acting monogamously or without IV drug use). In addition, the fact that the person did not know about the behavior of the other person indicates a kind of blindness and can be interpreted as a fundamental threat to self-esteem. These concerns are discussed more in depth next.

GENDER AND SAFER SEX IN HETEROSEXUAL RELATIONSHIPS

Examining safer sex from a communication perspective is important, particularly when considering the script often followed in heterosexual dating contexts. In a meta-analysis examining safer sex behavior in heterosexual couples, Allen et al. (2002) found that men and women who discussed condom use prior to having sex were more likely to actually use condoms during sex than individuals who did not engage in such conversations. Specifically, the authors found a 38% increase in condom use during sex due to such conversations. Implications of this finding are germane to working such conversations into men's and women's sexual scripts.

As of 2000, 38% of women who had AIDS reported acquiring HIV heterosexually (CDC, 2003a), whereas 25% of women had acquired HIV through IV drug use. Many women who acquired HIV heterosexually were infected by an IV drug-using partner. The incidence of HIV and AIDS is more pronounced in the Hispanic and Black populations. Of all the AIDS cases reported to the CDC through 2001, Blacks and Hispanics accounted for 57% of the total, 78% of the women, 79% of the heterosexuals (most of whom were infected from an IV drug using partner), and 82% of the children (CDC, 2003b).

On a positive note, Allen et al. (2002) found that women were more likely than men to introduce safer sex conversations. The authors also concluded that educational interventions focusing on taking a safer sex discussion initiative to be more effective with females than males. Of concern, however, is how women in heterosexual relationships introduce safer sex issues and *follow through* such that safer sex behaviors are practiced.

Although some research indicates that women might be more proactive in terms of date initiation (Perper & Weis, 1987), most research indicates that many heterosexual dating situations still follow the traditional sexual script (e.g., Byers, 1996; Check & Malamuth, 1983). The traditional sexual dating framework is concerning in some respects because it assumes a one-up/ one-down power differential between men and women, a script in which men make the decisions and the women follow. Byers (1996) argued that the traditional sexual script rewards men for being sexually active and penalizes women, by suggesting that she is promiscuous. Byers further advanced that the societal norms are as such that women's value is increased if she is involved in a relationship and that she must delicately balance engaging in enough sexual activity to keep her partner interested but not so much so that her reputation is called into question.

Conflicting findings exist regarding how women address safer sex issues in heterosexual dating relationships. For example, as mentioned, Allen et al. (2002) found that women were more likely to initiate safer sex discussions than men. Among HIV infected women reflecting on their attitudes and beliefs prior to their positive serostatus, however, Crowell and Emmers-Sommer (2001) found that women were more likely than men to believe that their partner was safe. Other research on safer sex has found that women were less argumentative than men (Crowell & Emmers-Sommer, 2000). These findings suggest a possible recipe for disaster. Specifically, women in heterosexual relationships are more likely to perceive a partner as safe, are less likely to argue for a condom, and are more inclined to follow a man's lead in the relationship, as dictated by the traditional sexual script.

A woman's introduction of condom use into discussion in a heterosexual relationship is not synonymous with actual usage. Although the woman is the ultimate gatekeeper in this context (i.e., "Wear a condom or no sex"), it is unclear how often women offer or follow through with this ultimatum. As indicated at the beginning of the chapter, introduction of safer sex discussion is a delicate situation. Implications exist if a woman does introduce safer sex discussion into the fray, as it suggests that sex could take place if a certain conditions are met (e.g., talk of sexual histories, use of condoms, etc.; Allen et al., 2002). Furthermore, and related to actual sexual situations, one must ask how women can initiate sexual discussions and protect their health without finding themselves in a psychologically or physically coercive situation (Allen et al., 2002). The classic question asked by one person of another, "do you love me?" indicates the need to provide a behavioral test of that love. The impact of this kind of statement is a kind of emotional blackmail or coercion because it ties an emotional state to a challenge for the individual to provide proof. Indeed, many women succumb to such forms of coercion and thus, risk their health as a result. These forms of coercion, as they relate to (un)safe sex, are addressed next.

Psychological Coercion

Coercion need not be presented in a violent form. That is, several forms of nonviolent coercion exist. Examples of nonviolent coercion include assumptions about the nature of sex and relationships, compulsory heterosexuality, status coercion, economic coercion, alcohol and drugs, and fear of male violence (to name a few; Muehlenhard & Schrag, 1991). Similar to Byers' (1996) contention that the same attitudes and behaviors exhibited by men and women are perceived differently by society (e.g., he is a "stud", she is a "slut"), research shows that women who initiate dates, pay for dates, go to a man's home and/or invite a man to her home are perceived more sexually by men (e.g., Bostwick & De Lucia, 1992; Mongeau & Carey, 1996; Muehlenhard, 1988; Muehlenhard, Friedman, & Thomas, 1985).

Research also finds that women often give in to sex due to constant badgering and encouragement by a male partner (Koss, Gidycz, & Wisniewski, 1987; Muehlenhard & Schrag, 1991). Similarly, unwanted sex and coercion are more likely to occur if women were intoxicated at the time of the encounter (e.g., Emmers-Sommer, 2002; Emmers-Sommer & Allen, 1999; Koss, 1988). Furthermore, research indicates that men often use alcohol and drugs to entice unwilling partners (e.g., Christopher & Frandsen, 1990). Problematically, men, and even women, might not perceive the unwanted sexual episode as coercive because judgment was blinded for each party due to intoxicants. Moreover, those who hold rape-myth related attitudes often perceive a woman who allows herself to get intoxicated and then has unwanted sex as "getting what she deserves" and men who engage in sexual acts under such conditions as not accountable for their actions (Burt, 1980).

Within the context of safer sex, these aforementioned situations are concerning because it is questionable whether or not safer sex practices are being exercised when sex is carried out in this fashion. For women to protect themselves, being an active participant in sex is not enough. Rather, women need to be proactive participants—making their wishes known and making it clear that sex will not occur if safer sex conditions are not met. Empowering women in this fashion is addressed in the next section.

Safer Sex Compliance-gaining

As indicated earlier in this book, the majority of the research presented in this text is specific to relationships in Western cultures. In less developed nations, many of which involve patriarchal societies, women have few rights and certainly little say in terms of sexual needs, wants, or health. Nonetheless, in more developed nations—and as reviewed earlier—many women feel oppressed due to social, sexual, or economic constraints. Within the context of safer sex, it is important for women to ask for a condom and to feel like they have the *right* to ask. Given that women are often socialized to be the relational harmonizers and gatekeepers in relationships, it is unfortunate to think that many women would prioritize the face saving of a partner over her own physical and sexual health. All too often, women feel as though they are "embarrassing the other person," "calling their own reputation into question," or fear that the partner will become upset with them for broaching the topics of safer sex, sexual history discussion, or condom use. The adage, "No one is going to care about you if you don't care about you" rings true, particularly in this context.

Given that women are typically the relational and sexual gatekeepers in relationships (Allen et al., 2002), women are put into a potential position of power and they might not even realize it. Specifically, women are in the position to make their wishes known regarding safer sexual practices and insist that they are followed or no sexual activity will occur. The issue is empowering women to seek and gain the compliance that they are seeking. Allen et al. (2002) argued, "... it is expected that individuals, and especially a woman's level of assertiveness, should have a direct impact on communication regarding condom use and hence actual condom use" (pp. 273–274). The CDC (2003a) emphasized that prevention programs need to be geared at women, because infection among women between the ages of 13 to 24 is increasing. The CDC went on to report that many women are unaware of their partners' risk factors and that, when tracked, over half of the women for who risk was initially unidentified were later reclassified as heterosexual transmission (CDC, 2003a).

Allen et al. (2002) suggest empowering individuals to exercise individual assertiveness on sexual issues. The authors argue that, "... assertiveness is likely to be a key variable in the complex social interaction of discussing condom use" (Treffke, Tiggemann, & Ross, 1992, as cited in Allen et al., 2002, p. 273). Research suggests that communication assertiveness training within the context of safer sex and condom use to be successful (e.g., Edgar, Freimuth, Hammond, McDonald, & Fink, 1992). Adelman (1992) suggested incorporating eroticism into safer sex talk as a means of introducing necessary measures without "ruining the moment." Breakwell, Fife-Schaw and Clayden (1991) found that perceived control over sexual relationships and the perceived ability to use condoms predicted intentions. The authors went on to indicate that when individuals believed they had no control over condom use or even the relationship, that their intentions to use a condom decreased. The problem of empowerment indicates that HIV infection will probably follow patterns related to power differentials in the relationships, meaning that women in positions of lowest power in society will probably be most as risk for infection.

Similarly, although much focus is on women in this portion of the chapter, it is important to also empower men such that they do not feel the need to have sex or "conquer"—a social pressure bestowed on men, aligned with the traditional sexual script. Indeed, men can engage in unwanted sexual activity as well as they can succumb to pressure to perform out of fear that they will not be perceived as manly or perhaps as homosexual (Emmers-Sommer, 2002).

CONCLUSION

The purpose of this chapter was to examine safer sexual discussions and practices in heterosexual dating relationships. As indicated, unique features of this relationship type can make such discussions difficult. Moreover, from a theoretical standpoint, these conversations and practices are often deemed as unnecessary as such behaviors are coupled with homosexual, and not heterosexual, populations. It is of utmost importance that individuals in the heterosexual population personalize HIV risk and take appropriate steps to lessen the risk. To do so, men and women must realize that several factors contributing to men's and women's sense of invulnerability as well as their condom nonuse are in error. Research should continue to examine assertiveness and actual (versus intentional) compliance gaining as well as the personal and social responses to such practices. If such conversations can be woven into the social and political fabric, it is expected that the awkwardness, discomfort, and taboo nature of such conversations will diminish.

The problems of understanding heterosexual dating and HIV infection must provide a connection between information, relational development, and power between partners. Persons lacking a sense of power will not be able to assert and gain compliance in safer sexual practices. At the same time, the definition of relationships is tied to trust and monogamy. The problem is that such a definition or perception puts persons at risk when one partner does not share that value. When this lack of shared practice is combined with power differentials between partners, the determination of which partner gets to define the level of safety or relational achievement puts one partner clearly more at risk. The current assumptions about relational trajectory and practices indicate a long-term heterosexual population continuing to be at risk.

Safer Sex and Marriage

Tara M. Emmers-Sommer
University of Arizona

Tara L. Crowell
The Richard Stockton College of New Jersey

Mike Allen
University of Wisconsin-Milwaukee

As indicated in chapter One, a marked increase exists in the numbers of individuals acquiring AIDS through heterosexual contact. Although research on individuals at risk (e.g., bisexual men, gay men, IV drug users) remains warranted (and reports of increases are sometimes noted), the aforementioned research findings suggest that some persons may to be at "low-to-no risk." This perception may be shared by society and the sexual partners of the person. One such group considered in this chapter is individuals that are married.

Spouses often perceive little to no risk of contracting HIV due to their relational status (Crowell & Emmers-Sommer, 2001; Ellen, Vittinghoff, Bolan, Boyer, & Padian, 1998; Willing, 1994). Individuals in marital relationships typically view themselves involved in committed, higher-level relationship than those in nonmarital relationships (Knapp & Taylor, 1994). With that perceived "safety and security" generated in what many consider to be an exclusive heterosexual partnership (at the current time law does not permit homosexual marriage) comes a perceived safety and immunity from sexually transmitted diseases (Willing, 1994). Sexually transmitted diseases become something associated with those in noncommitted, nonsexually exclusive relationships that involve either casual or commercial sexual encounters. Yet, a review of various recent studies on extramarital infidelity suggests that 15% to 25% of married individuals engage in adultery (Wiederman, 1997). A paucity of research on safer sex in marriage exists; yet, for a large number of spouses, the risk of HIV is real. For example, recent research (Crowell & Emmers-Sommer, 2001) on heterosexuals who acquired HIV through heterosexual sex indicates that many of the participants acquired the virus from a spouse, fiancé or fiancée, cohabiting partner, or serious relational partner. The majority of Crowell and Emmers-Sommer's sample (N = 40) reported not discussing safer sexual issues and not engaging in safer sex with their spouse or partner because they assumed that they were "safe" given their relational status. Unfortunately, they misperceived their "safety" and eventually unknowingly acquired HIV from their unfaithful partner. To be exact, 75% of the individuals who answered the question regarding acquisition of the virus had acquired the virus from their partner. Many of the participants reported that although their partner's admittance of infidelity might have been devastating to them, it would have been far less devastating than learning that they had acquired a virus that lead to a terminal disease from an unfaithful partner.

This chapter examines safer sex discussions and practices within the context of marriage. To do so, extant literature is reviewed and a study conducted on safer sex in marriage is offered. This chapter offers insight into spouses' willingness to discuss sexual histories and practices that might put each another at risk and the implications of such discussion on the maintenance of the relationship. In doing so, the notion of a marital script is examined as well as various factors that influence condom (non) use within the context of marriage. By legal definition, this approach only considers heterosexuals, although many of the same fundamental issues are reflected in committed relationships between persons that are not married. However, given that marriage is a recognizable social institution with centuries of developed and expected social practices, the development of routines or expected routines exists for this particular status.

Condom Use

One specific behavior reducing individuals' risk of acquiring HIV and other forms of sexually transmitted diseases is the use of condoms (Katz, Fortenberry, Zimet, Blyth, & Orr, 2000). Although condoms are not 100% effective in preventing HIV transmission, they do substantially reduce the risk (Emmers-Sommer & Allen, 2001; Reiss & Leik, 1989). For example, Reiss and Leik (1989) tested two behavioral possibilities regarding lowering HIV acquisition: reducing the number of partners and using condoms. The authors found that "consistent and careful condom use is a far more effective method of reducing HIV infection than is reducing the number of sexual partners" (p. 411). Yet, research indicates that individuals in exclusive relationships (i.e., exclusively seeing one partner) used condoms significantly less than those in nonexclusive relationships (i.e., not seeing anyone in particular regularly; e.g., Crowell & Emmers-Sommer, 2000, 2001; Metts & Fitzpatrick, 1992). In a study examining sexual behavior in college undergraduates, for example, Critelli and Suire (1998) found that individuals in casual relationships used condoms significantly more (i.e., 59.6%) than individuals involved in more serious, monogamous relationships (i.e., 43.2%).

Given the higher level of commitment associated with marriage by the individual, it is likely that marital partners use condoms even less than those in exclusive dating relationships. This assertion is advanced for several reasons. First, Metts and Fitzpatrick (1992) argued that condom use tends to wane as relationship levels advance to more serious and committed stages. Indeed, relationships that have achieved the level of marriage experience more commitment than a seriously dating or casual relationship (e.g., Knapp & Taylor, 1994). Second, as relationships advance, condoms often diminish or completely disappear as a mode of birth control in favor of other forms (e.g., the pill; e.g., Lear, 1995; Maticka-Tyndale, 1991; Metts & Fitzpatrick, 1992).

Reasons for Not Using Condoms

Numerous investigations have yielded common reasons for not using condoms among sexually active individuals. The following are six reasons for non-condom use, each of which is influenced by personal, situational, and/or relational factors. First, many individuals, especially those involved in romantic relationships, perceive condoms as birth control devices rather than a means for preventing sexually transmitted diseases (Metts & Fitzpatrick, 1992). Thus, if alternative methods of birth control are being practiced, condoms are perceived as unnecessary. The focus of condom use becomes not STD reduction but instead reflects contraception. The change in birth control to other devices may reflect the expectation of a regular partner and relationship that requires planning (like taking a pill), the desire to reduce barriers, make sex become more natural or special, as well as more practical.

Second, many individuals have negative attitudes toward condoms (Brown, 1984). Sonnex, Hart, Williams, and Adler (1989) report the following as barriers to condom use: reduced sensitivity, loss of spontaneity during intercourse, discomfort, unpleasant odor, and messiness. After ejacu- lation the condom should be removed while the penis is erect, the after sex actions may be viewed as less favorable and detract from a focus on the person in the act of sex.

A third reason for not using condoms considers alcohol or drug use: Studies suggest that alcohol or drug use may impact individuals' judgment and choices, and thus, they may perceive a partner as "safe" and rationalize that as an excuse for not using a condom (Carroll & Carroll, 1995). This psychological reaction comes from beliefs that the current partner is the "one," and that a long-term or even lifelong relationship is emerging that offers safety.

Fourth, decisions regarding condom use are affected by perceived need for the use of condoms. Men and women often perceive little, if any, need to use a condom because they believe they are already engaging in safer sex by choosing a partner who is "safe" (Ishii-Kuntz et al., 1990). Individuals believe that "unsafe" people are somehow distinguishable from safe people, and therefore, they can be recognized and avoided as sexual partners (Ishii-Kuntz et al., 1990; Metts & Fitzpatrick, 1992).

A fifth reason is individuals' feelings of invincibility. Many individuals perceive themselves to be at low risk in terms of acquiring HIV. These attitudes may play a substantive role in individuals' enacting risky sexual behaviors (Ehde et al., 1995). This view is also undermined by the emergence of increasingly effective means of treating HIV and the opportunistic infections that emerge. As survivability rates improve, the fear of the disease reduces and this would increase the sense of invincibility.

The sixth reason for not using condoms considers relational factors. Specifically, studies have found that when partners indicate they trust each other, feel more positively about their partner and the relationship, and have like/love and commitment for their partner, they were less likely to use condoms and less concerned about AIDS and STDs (Adam, Sears, & Schellenberg, 2000; Ishii-Kuntz et al., 1990; Pilkington et al., 1994). Theoretically, the marital script enacted by spouses typically does not include discussion of safer sex or practices that might have or will put the other spouse at risk. This notion is further explored next.

Relational Scripts

Regarding relationships, three types of scripts exist: (a) cultural scenarios, (b) interpersonal scripts, and, (c) intrapsychic scripts (Hynie et al., 1998). Cultural scenarios are societal, cultural, or subcultural scripts regarding social expectations about sexual behavior, the relationship between partners, and appropriateness of activity. Interpersonal scripts involve an individual's understanding of cultural scenarios and how he or she combines that understanding with his or her own desires and the current situation. Intrapsychic scripts "are the internalization of the socially shared scripts and scenarios" (p. 371).

Hynie et al. (1998) examined the extent to which safer sex was incorporated into women's relational scripts in nonmarried samples, arguing that if women's relational scripts did not include condom use they would experience difficulty negotiating safer sex. Results of Hynie et al.'s investigation finds that scripts involving condom use were perceived as less relational than those with condom nonuse and that support for the relational ideal was related to less positive attitudes toward condoms and lesser likelihood of use. Overall, findings indicate that safer sex attitudes and behavior are negatively related to relational ideals in nonmarried samples. From a script theory perspective, safer sex attitudes and behaviors are more likely to be excluded from marital relational scripts given the perceived exclusivity and relational idealism associated with marriage (Knapp & Taylor, 1994).

Marriage and "Safety"

Marriage represents an institution whereby men and women are joined in a special kind of social and legal interdependence (Knapp & Taylor, 1994). Typically, men and women who agree to enter into marriage do so with a partner they love, trust, and hope to build a future with. The bond of marriage usually brings with it a high degree of commitment, trust, and openness between partners. The words "till death do us part," while not true in reality (50% of marriages end in divorce) represent an ideal or desired outcome sought by the two persons.

Most spouses hold the belief that the mere nature of marriage provides a safe haven from acquiring HIV or STDs (Willing, 1994). Specifically, Willing (1994) argued how this sense of security comes about: "First, a reference to a person's marital status was presented as sufficient grounds for an assumption of safety and/or immunity in relation to the possibility of HIV infection. Second, it was suggested that spouses are required to trust each other and are therefore obliged to assume that they are safe" (p. 113).

In addition to the nature of marriage, the duration of marriage tends to increase this perception of safety. Specifically, individuals often report lack of condom use because of the perceived safety experienced due to the duration of their marriage (Willing, 1994). The assumption of a married partner is that the longer the period of marriage, the greater the evidence of commitment and stability. This assumption is combined with the belief that the sexual relationship is an exclusive one, then the safety is actual if the behavior actually is true (insofar as sexually transmitted HIV is concerned). The importance of fidelity in the relationship is confirmed because a long lasting marriage should reflect the underlying behavioral script.

Trust

Trust is a crucial defining feature within interpersonal relationships (friendships, marriages, long-term partners, dating, etc.) and an important construct for understanding the development of and communication in personal relationships (Couch & Jones, 1997; Larzelere & Huston, 1980). O'Neil and O'Neil (cited in Larzelere & Huston, 1980) posited that trust is a prerequisite for marital partners in order for them to be open in their marriage and reach full optimal personal and interpersonal growth. In addition, other findings suggest that trust becomes essential for the development of intimacy in romantic relationships (Burgoon & Hale, 1987; Hendrick & Hendrick, 1992), correlated with love (Rempel, Holmes, & Zanna, 1985), and affects intimate self-disclosure (Steel, 1991).

Individuals often report "trusting their partner" as a reason for not using a condom (Crowell & Emmers-Sommer, 2001). Within the context of marriage, Willing (1994) found that the request to use a condom could undermine trust, insult the partner, and thus damage the relationship. A spouse requesting the use of condom would probably receive a series of questions from the other spouse, many of the questions probably reflecting fears of a sexual relationship with another person.

Although trust in a relationship is supposed to precipitate and encourage open communication, the suggestion to use a condom contradicts these assumptions. Willing (1994) argued that "not talking about things and not asking certain questions, is much more fundamental to the development and maintenance of a trusting relationship than to talk honesty and openly" (p. 117). Thus, the influence trust has on communication within a sexual context may be very different than trust in a more general interpersonal context.

Intimacy

Intimacy is another construct that plays an important role in the development and maintenance of interpersonal relationships. Marston, Hecht, Manke, McDaniel, and Reeder (1998) reported that the research on intimacy has focused on three components: (a) the ways in which relational partners reveal information on private topics (i.e., self-disclosure); (b) the ways in which partners communicate affection; and, (c) the ways in which partners develop interdependent behavioral patterns. Many researchers who have studied intimacy reveal that the following are influential in establishing and maintaining intimacy: the expression of emotion (Wegscheider-Cruse, 1988), informational disclosure (Fitzpatrick, 1987), communication of affection (Helgeson, Shaver, & Dryer, 1987) and spending time together (Hatfield & Rapson, 1987).

The relationship between intimacy and condom use suggestion is yet to be determined. Logically, it would seem that the more intimacy perceived between two people, the greater the probability that these two individuals feel close enough to self-disclose their feelings or concerns regarding anything (Altman & Taylor, 1973). However, suggestions to talk about condom use may threaten the integrity of the relationship (Willing, 1994). Hence, despite a feeling of closeness, broaching the subject of condom use, or safer sex in general, might have negative implications.

Given the previous review regarding aspects of marriage, it is expected that condom use suggestion introduced into a marital relationship will impact trust and intimacy. In gay relationships, for example, trust and intimacy are negatively related to condom use (Adam et al., 2000). However, the explanation a partner offers with his or her condom use suggestion is also expected to impact the reception of the suggestion. That is, if the manner of suggestion is perceived by one or both partners as a violation of their relational script, it will be perceived negatively (Metts, 1994). Considering the previous review, the following hypotheses and research questions are offered:

H1   Condom use negatively relates to number of years married.

H2   Type of condom request scenario relates to intimacy such that the "infidelity" scenario has the most negative impact on intimacy.

H3   Type of condom request scenario relates to trust such that the "infidelity" has the most negative impact on trust.

RQ1   How prevalent is condom use in marital relationships?

RQ2   What are reasons for condom non-use in marriage?

RQ3   How many married adults perceive condoms as lowering risk of STD transmission as opposed to perceiving them primarily as birth control devices?

RQ4   How do married individuals respond to condom use suggestion in their marriage?

METHOD

Data Collection and Instrumentation

Participants were solicited from several general education courses, representing a diversity of majors, at a large university in the south central United States. In order to participate in the study, individuals had to be married and both the individual and his or her marital partner had to be willing to complete the survey at Time 1 and Time 2. Unmarried individuals passed the questionnaire packets on at Time 1 and Time 2 to a married couple they knew. Written instructions were provided in the couple-packets at Time 1 and at Time 2. Instructions were read aloud in the classes for the married participants and for the benefit of unmarried individuals who would also pass the packets on to their married acquaintances. In addition, written instructions were provided in each packet that reiterated the oral instructions given in class. Time 1 and Time 2 instructions are as follows:

(a) Read and sign the consent form.

(b) Wives—fill out the questionnaire marked "F" for female. Husbands, fill out the questionnaire marked "M" for male. You will each get an accompanying white envelope for your questionnaire. Fill out your questionnaire INDE-PENDENTLY from your spouse. When you are done, put your questionnaire into your respective white envelope, SEAL IT, SIGN YOUR NAME OVER THE SEAL, and put your white envelope into the big, manila envelope. When your spouse has also added his or her sealed and signed white envelope to the big, ma-nila envelope, please RETURN IT TO THE RESEARCHERS OR YOUR IN-STRUCTOR IMMEDIATELY.

Participants' signatures over their sealed envelope served as a reliability check to the researchers that the participants completed the questionnaires as opposed to the individual who passed it on to them. Similar to the method used by Emmers and Dindia (1995), signatures were examined to ensure that they were not similar or odd (e.g., both were signed in purple pen, etc.).

Time 1 Questionnaire. The Time 1 questionnaire included demographic questions regarding age, sex, years married, number of sexual encounters with the spouse per week, prevalence of condom use, types of birth control used, reasons for not using condoms, who initiates conversations about con-traceptive use, willingness to support a spouse's request to use a condom, self and partner fidelity, and self and partner experience with STDs.

Trust

Participants' trust for their partner was operationalized by using their scores to the Larzelere and Huston's (1980) Dyadic Trust Scale. The scale offers eight items addressing the amount of trust an individual experiences about his or her partner on a 1 to 7 scale (1 = completely disagree, 7 = completely agree). The scale demonstrates construct validity and past reliability coeffi-cients for the scale range from .72 to .89 (Cronbach's alpha) (Larzelere & Huston, 1980). Reliability for the scale with this sample at Time 1 was .70 (Cronbach's alpha). Reliability of the Dyadic Trust Scale at Time 2 was .85.

Intimacy

Intimacy was operationalized by examining participants' responses to the Miller Social Intimacy Scale (MSIS) (Miller & Lefcourt, 1982). The MSIS measures psychological closeness in dyadic and romantic relationships. The MSIS demonstrates concurrent and discriminant validity (Baxter, 1988). Reliability coefficients for the scale range from .86 to .91 (Miller & Lefcourt) The reliability coefficient with this sample was acceptable (Cronbach's alpha = .89). Reliability of the Miller Social Intimacy Scale at Time 2 was .92.

Time 2 Questionnaire. Three weeks after the collection of the completed Time 1 questionnaires, Time 2 questionnaires were distributed to the same sample. At Time 2, participants were randomly assigned to one of three possible scenarios. To create hypothetical scenarios, the authors relied on past literature regarding reasons for condom use. From this, the authors created three hypothetical scenarios: Scenario 1—No explanation; Scenario 2—Pregnancy explanation; and, Scenario 3—Infidelity explanation.

Scenario One

Participants who received Scenario One were presented with the following: "Your spouse approaches you and says, 'I think we should start using condoms whenever we want to have sexual intercourse.'" Participants then completed the same measures regarding trust and intimacy. Participants were then presented with the scenario once again and asked to respond to an open-ended question instructing them to identify and describe how they would react to their spouse's disclosure.

Scenario Two

Participants who received Scenario Two were presented with the following: "Your spouse approaches you and says, 'I think we should start using condoms whenever we want to have sexual intercourse. We both know that a pregnancy right now would be bad for us and condoms are a reliable primary or backup method of birth control.'" Participants then completed the same measures regarding trust and intimacy. Participants were then presented with the scenario once again and asked to respond to an open-ended question instructing them to identify and describe how they would react to their spouse's disclosure.

Scenario Three

Participants who received Scenario Three were presented with the following: "Your spouse approaches you and says, 'I think we should start using condoms whenever we want to have sexual intercourse. I've been unfaithful.'" Participants then completed the same measures regarding trust and intimacy. Participants were then presented with the scenario once again and asked to respond to an open-ended question instructing them to identify and describe how they would react to their spouse's disclosure.

Participants

Overall, 352 husbands and wives participated in the study ($n = 176$ couples). The average age was 33.3 ($SD = 11.65$) with an age range of 18-74. The average years married was 9.8 years ($SD = 10.43$) with a range of 1 year or less to 51 years. Regarding infidelity in their marriages, 6.8% reported that they had extramarital affairs and 4.2% reported that they were aware of their partner cheating. Seven percent reported "not knowing" if their spouse has cheated or not. Only 4.2% reported using a condom with the secondary partner during the extramarital sexual episode(s). Regarding sexually transmitted diseases, approximately 6% of the sample reported that during the duration of their marriage, they had or currently have an STD, while the other 94% reported that they did not. Considering their spouse, approximately 5% of the sample indicated that their partner had or has an STD. Ninety percent reported that their partner did not have an STD and approximately 5% reported that they did not know if their partner has or had an STD. Regarding sexual practices, participants reported a mode of "one" regarding how many times per week they had sexual intercourse with their spouse. Only 10% of the sample reported that they would "refuse to have sex with their spouse if he/she requested using a condom" while the remainder of the sample reported willingness to grant their partner's wish to use a condom. Twelve percent reported actually experiencing that situation. Twenty-one percent of the sample reported that they initiated conversations about condoms in their marriage, 19% reported that their partner initiated discussions about condoms, 55% reported that "no one" initiated such discussions, and three percent reported "both." Two percent of the sample did not answer the question. Regarding alternative birth control, 35.4% reported using "the pill," 22.9% of the men and women in the sample reported "sterilization." Given the average age and age range in this study, the number of sterilized participants was not surprising. Research indicates that men and their women in their 30's often rely on sterilization as a birth control technique. Specifically, 15-20% of men in this age group undergo a vasectomy and 24% of men in this age group and 31% of women in this age group rely on female sterilization as a birth control technique (The Alan Guttmacher Institute, 2002). Other research indicates that sterilization is often an election of women aged 30 and younger (Hillis,

Marchbanks, Tylor, & Peterson, 1999) and that, overall, sterilization is the most widely used form of birth control in the United States (Spinelli, Talamanca, & Lauria, 2000). Just over 2% (2.3%) reported "withdrawal" or the "rhythm method," respectively, 1.4% reported "spermicide," 2% reported "Depovera," and 33.4% did not answer the question.

Mode sex per week was reported versus the mean because of a few extreme reportings. Average sex per week was 2.8 and the range was 1 to 25 time(s) per week.

RESULTS

Research Question One

Research Question One asked, "How prevalent is condom use in marital relationships?" Participants reported how often they used condoms during sex in their marriage (1 = never, 2 = rarely, 3 = sometimes, 4 = half the time, 5 = most times, 6 = almost all times, 7 = always). Eighty-three percent of the sample reported using condoms "less than half of the time." A total of 64% of the respondents reported that they "never" used condoms. Only 16% of the sample reported using condoms "half of the time or more" and only 7.6% reported that they always used condoms. The average reported condom use was 2.13 (i.e., "rarely"). The results indicate that married couples are rarely consistent condom users and the majority of married couples never use a condom.

Research Question Two

Research Question Two asked, "What are reasons for condom non-use in marriage?" Responses to the open-ended question were initially coded by the first author. Inspired by research using similar coding procedures (e.g., Emmers & Canary, 1996), categories were created to correspond with each reason. When a reason arose that did not correspond to an existing category, a new category was created. An outside coder, uniformed as to the nature of the study, served as the reliability check; reliability was acceptable, with Cohen's kappa = .81.

Seventy-five percent of the sample answered this question, and 49% gave "relational reasons" for not always using a condom during sex (e.g., monogamy, trust, commitment, exclusivity). Examples include, "My spouse and I are married, we don't need to use condoms," or "We're in a monogamous, committed marriage, we don't cheat." Nearly 39% reported using "alternative birth control" as a reason for not using condoms. Less than 1% reported reasons of feeling "invulnerable." Six percent reported having a bad experience/bad attitude as a reason for not using a condom, and 3% reported "wanting to get pregnant" as a reason for not using a condom. Only 1% reported miscellaneous reasons (e.g., "birth control is against my religion"). The basis for lack of condom use is seldom related to the desire to have children, the reason for lack of condom use is primarily related to the belief that using a condom represents a sign of trust and commitment.

Research Question Three

Research Question Three asked, "How many married adults perceive condoms as lowering risk of STD transmission as opposed to perceiving them primarily as birth control devices?" Participants responded to a question asking them what immediate perceptions they had at the mention of "condoms." Ninety-six percent of the sample reported immediately associating condoms with "birth control" whereas only 4% immediately acknowledged their utility as reducing the risk of acquiring HIV or other STDs. This finding is consistent with most earlier research that suggests the use of a condom represents contraception and not STD prevention for unmarried heterosexuals.

Hypothesis One

Hypothesis One argued, "Condom use negatively relates to number of years married." H1 was supported, $r = -.24, p < .01$. Therefore, the longer a couple is married, the less likely they are to use a condom with their spouse.

Hypothesis Two

To analyze H2 and H3, husbands' and wives' trust and intimacy scores were first compared to see if they were significantly different in order to determine how to proceed. Hypothesis Two posited, "Type of condom request scenario relates to intimacy such that the 'infidelity' scenario has the most negative impact on intimacy." Results of paired t-tests revealed that intimacy and trust were significantly different at Time 1, $t = -51.490, p < .001$ and at Time 2, $t = -37.953, p < .001$. H2 was tested with a oneway ANOVA and was supported, $F = 3.22$, eta $= .02, p < .04$. Post hoc Tukey HSD tests indicated that participants who received the "infidelity" condition reported significantly less intimacy than those who received the "no explanation" condition. An analysis of intimacy means across groups indicated a descent from Scenario 1 ("No Explanation") $(M = 8.01)$ to Scenario 2 ("Pregnancy Explanation") $(M = 7.94)$ to Scenario Three ("Infidelity Explanation") $(M = 7.66)$. Similarly, a paired t-test revealed that intimacy at Time 2 $(M = 7.88)$ was significantly lower than intimacy reported at Time 1 $(M = 8.09)$, $t = 3.84, p < .001$.

Degrees of freedom represent attrition from Time 1 to Time 2 as well as some respondents' failure to answer the question.

Hypothesis Three

Hypothesis Three contended, "Type of condom request scenario relates to trust such that the 'infidelity' scenario has the most negative impact on trust." H3 was supported, $F = 8.23$, eta $= .05$, $p < .001$. Post hoc Tukey HSD tests revealed that participants receiving the "No Explanation" scenario reported significantly less trust ($M = 5.43$) than those who received the "Pregnancy Explanation" ($M = 5.80$) and those who received the "Pregnancy Explanation" reported significantly more trust than those who received the "Infidelity Explanation" ($M = 5.15$). Thus, receiving an explanation that was deemed as "acceptable" (i.e., pregnancy prevention) seemed to impact trust more positively whereas an "unacceptable" explanation (i.e., infidelity) was perceived more negatively than "no explanation" at all. Nevertheless, results to H3 should be interpreted with caution because results of a paired t-test revealed that trust scores significantly *increased* from Time 1 ($M = 5.02$) to Time 2 ($M = 5.47$), $t = 6.52$, $p < .001$. This unexpected finding is addressed later in the discussion section.

Research Question Four

Research Question Four asked, "How do married individuals respond to condom use suggestion in their marriage?" Once again, categories were created to correspond with each reason. When a reason arose that did not correspond to an existing category, a new category was created. An outside coder, uniformed as to the nature of the study, served as the reliability check; Cohen's kappa $= .80$.

Ten percent of the sample did not provide a response to how they would react to their partner's suggestion of condom use. Of the 90% who did respond, 44% reported that they would "comply/accept/work it out" with their partner's request. Twenty-one percent reported that they would feel "suspicious/upset/angry/betrayed." Six percent reported that it was "not an issue" for various reasons (e.g., they already were pregnant, they wanted to get pregnant, they were sterilized). Approximately 6% reported that they would ask "why?" and 13.6% reported that they would "leave/divorce." Five percent reported "it would never happen to us," and 3.8% reported that they would "refuse to comply or abstain" from sex. Finally, approximately 1% reported miscellaneous responses to the condom request (e.g., hit partner, cheat themselves, did not mind because partner likely chose a "safe" person). As a follow up, responses to the scenario were compared to the scenario received. A chi-square test of independence could not be conducted due to cells < 7 for some of the response categories because not all participants answered the question. Nevertheless, for those respondents who did answer the question, an examination of cell frequencies indicated that participants who received the "pregnancy explanation" were most likely to respond to the condom request with "comply/accept/work it out." Participants who received the "no explanation" treatment most often reported a response of "suspicious/upset/angry/betrayed." Finally, participants who were in the "infidelity" group were most likely to respond to a condom request with "leave/divorce."

What the results demonstrate is a legitimate concern for someone that would want to use a condom in a marriage when previously not used. The responses indicate that the perception of the issue raised by a spouse becomes an admission of infidelity and even challenges the fundamental nature of the relationship. The couple has developed an explicit and probably unstated procedure for sexual conduct that does not require a condom. The introduction of the topic or request, for a substantial portion of the sample, indicates a relational violation and loss of trust. The script or pattern of behavior that does not have a condom used during sex stems from an implicit relational definition, a change in status is a perception of a change in the definition of the relationship.

DISCUSSION

Results indicate that only 16% of the participants report using condoms half of the time or more and only 7.6% report always using condoms. The majority of the participants, 64%, report never using condoms. These results are similar to past findings regarding condom use with unmarried individuals, revealing low levels of consistent condom use and moderate to high levels of no condom use (Brafford & Beck, 1991; Crowell & Emmers-Sommer, 2001). Relationship status impacts an individual's sense of invincibility (Crowell & Emmers-Sommer, 2000, 2001; Ishii-Kuntz et al., 1990; Metts & Fitzpatrick, 1992; Pilkington et al., 1994). This perceived invulnerability then influences individuals' use of condoms because they hold attitudes that distort their perceptions of condom necessity (e.g., Ehde et al., 1995; Ishii-Kuntz et al., 1990; Misovich, Fisher, & Fisher, 1997; Timmins et al., 1993), or that condom use does not relate to a relational ideal (Hynie et al., 1998). This study found similar results when participants were asked to provide reasons for a lack of condom use in their marriage.

Results reveal that participants indicated two major reasons for not using condoms in marriages; together accounting for almost 90% of all reasons. Relational reasons were the most frequently reported reasons why individuals did not use condoms. Individuals provided reasons such as being in a monogamous committed relationship, being married, and no one was cheating (to their knowledge), as justification for not needing to use condoms. These results are consistent with past findings, which indicate that individuals in exclusive and committed relationships report little to no condom use (Crowell & Emmers-Sommer, 2001; Ishii-Kuntz et al., 1990; Metts & Fitzpatrick, 1992). Individuals often believe that because they are married, or in an exclusive committed relationship, that the relational status makes them "safe." Individuals have even reported that the safest sex is with a "safe" partner (Metts & Fitzpatrick, 1992). Thus, perceived exclusive relational status and condom necessity may be perceived as mutually exclusive.

The second major reason participants report for not using a condom is "alternative birth control" (e.g., birth control pill). Almost 40% of the sample reported the use of alternative forms of birth control. Thus, if individuals are currently using alternative forms of birth control they perceive no need for condoms. Similarly, only 4% acknowledged condoms as a method of reducing HIV and other STDs. These findings reflect past results indicating that among heterosexual couples, condoms are primarily considered a method for birth control rather than a means for preventing sexually transmitted diseases (Maticka-Tyndale, 1991; Sonnex et al., 1989).

As expected, spouses have not incorporated discussions and practice of safer sex into their marital relational scripts. These potentially tainted perceptions of "safety" might affect discussion of safer sexual issues in the relationship. For example, a study of individuals and their main sexual partner, Ellen et al. (1998) found that participants misperceived their partner's risk behaviors and that many more partners had engaged in risky sexual behavior unbeknownst to the participant. Ellen et al. concluded that individuals were not asking about their partner's risky sexual behavior and/or were not being told the truth by their partner. As a result, many individuals were unknowingly in danger of acquiring HIV. Other research on infidelity and marriage also suggests that partners assume that a spouse is faithful and violation of that assumption relates to adverse emotions. Specifically, spouses often experience traumatic responses and feelings of betrayal upon learning of their partner's secret extramarital affair (Glass & Wright, 1997).

Specific to this study, perceptions of not needing to discuss safer sexual issues might hold great danger for individuals given each spouse's sexual history coming into the marriage as well as the occurrence of extramarital affairs.

Although results report infidelity for participants was only 11%, this statistic is lower than other nationally reported statistics for extramarital relations (Wiederman, 1997). There could be many reasons for these discrepancies: sensitive nature of the topic, omission of information, deception, perception of no confidentiality of the survey, or regional characteristics (e.g., data were collected in a more conservative region of the U.S.). However, whatever the reason, the reported number of infidelities found in this study illustrate two important points. First, out of the number of reported cases of infidelity, only 61% of partners were aware of their spouse's infidelity. Thus, 39% of the spouses who may perceive their partner as safe (due to their marital status and perceptions of a monogamous relationship) may have a false sense of security. Second, 39% of individuals who did cheat did not use condoms with their secondary partner. Again, illustrating that almost 40% of spouses who perceive their partner as "safe," because of relational reasons, may be more susceptible to acquiring HIV and other STDs than they believe. Individuals' perception of safety due to relational status also may be tied to the relationship that was found between condom use and years married.

Results reveal that participants receiving the "infidelity" condition report lower intimacy than those receiving the "pregnancy prevention" or "no explanation" condition. There was a significant difference in individuals' level of intimacy between individuals who received no explanation for condom use suggestion and for those who received the "infidelity" condition. These results support the perception that many individuals have of infidelity; specifically, although the research indicates that infidelity is fairly common in both marital and exclusive premarital relationships (Pittman, 1989; Roche & Ramsey 1993; Roscoe, Cavanaugh, & Kennedy, 1988; Thompson, 1983), it is generally perceived by many as a major rule violation (e.g., Metts, 1994).

The occurrence of infidelity by one or both partners has the potential to jeopardize the foundation on which many intimate relationships are built: trust. One study conducted by Spanier and Margolis (1983) reports that separated marital partners felt their partner's infidelity was a cause of the marital breakup. The present study found that participants receiving the "infidelity" condition report lower trust than those of the other two conditions. Thus, it appears that suggestion of condom use may not lower trust if it is a "socially acceptable reason" such as birth control.

Considering that marriage is one romantic relationship that many perceive as monogamous, regardless of actual rates of infidelity, trust in marriage may not always decrease due to external threats, such as suggestion of condoms or occurrences of infidelity. In the present study, trust actually increased between Time 1 to Time 2. This finding was unexpected. One possible, although not necessarily probable, explanation for this result is that individuals felt the need to reinforce their level of trust for their partner upon reading the hypothetical scenario. Recall, many individuals reported that their reason for not using condoms was that "there was no need." Most individuals reported that they trusted their partner and both they and their partner were faithful. Many respondents indicated that they just could not fathom the possibility of infidelity. Thus, when faced with a scenario that indicated that their partner had been unfaithful, participants had to reaffirm their original stance: "I trust my partner, we are faithful to each other, and we would never cheat on each other." Hence, although infidelity has the potential to threaten intimacy and trust in marital relationships, if individuals cannot personalize the potential of infidelity in their own marriage, trust will remain unaffected or even increase due to an existing halo effect about their spouse. This phenomenon did not occur with intimacy at Time 2. However, recall that intimacy and trust were not significantly correlated in this study. Nevertheless, further research is necessary to examine possible explanations for this unexpected outcome.

The final issue that this study addressed is how married individuals respond to condom use suggestion. Although findings varied by scenario, results reveal that the majority of individuals (44%) would "comply/accept, work out" a partner's request to use a condom. These results are consistent with past studies that found a positive relationship between request for condom use and actual condom use (Edgar, Freimuth, Hammond, McDonald, & Fink, 1992; Freimuth, Hammond, Edgar, McDonald, & Fink, 1992; Yesmont, 1992). Additionally, less than 4% of participants indicated that they would refuse to comply or abstain. What is suggested from the present and past findings is that individuals are willing to discuss condom use and comply with such requests, but often do not. Future research should examine what strategies partners use to effectively suggest condom use and the level of compliance associated with such strategies.

The second most frequent response reported was "suspicious/upset/angry/betrayed." Participants who were in the "no explanation" group were most likely to respond to condom requests in this manner. Considering that individuals were not given a reason for this suggestion, these feelings may not be due to the actual suggestion of condom use, but because of the lack of information they were provided. Research on romantic relationships indicates that trust and intimacy are positively correlated with self-disclosure (Steel, 1991). This adds support to why more individuals in the "pregnancy explanation" were more likely comply with condom use suggestion.

The third most frequent response individuals provide for partners' condom request is "leave or divorce." Participants who were in the infidelity group were more likely to report this response, which coincides with the decline of trust and intimacy of participants. Results reveal that only 6% of the participants indicated that they would ask "why?" if their partner requested to use a condom. This result appears to support the notion of trust in marriages. Considering that most spouses' level of trust is so high, they do not perceive a need to question their spouse. If marriage brings with it an underlying premise of fidelity, trust, commitment, and intimacy, issues such as condom use, may not have the same meaning they do in other romantic relationships.

FUTURE CONSIDERATIONS

While the findings of this investigation are valuable, results must be interpreted with the understanding that Time 1 responses involved actual perceptions of the relationship whereas Time 2 responses were based on reactions to hypothetical situations. With that said, the key purpose of this investigation was not to necessarily promote condom use in marriage. Rather, it was to examine spouses' communication about sexual histories and safer sex as well as their willingness to discuss safer sex in their marriage. Although the majority of spouses reported not discussing safer sex with their spouse or practicing it, the majority reported that they would be willing to entertain a condom use request from their spouse. Similarly, when faced with various condom use suggestion scenarios, spouses most frequently reported that they would be willing to comply and work out the request.

The lack of discussion of sexual histories and risk in marital relationships is potentially harmful if pre-existing conditions exist. Similarly, if risk behavior occurs during the course of a marriage (e.g., infidelity) and the offender does not disclose this to the spouse it could also pose a potential health risk. However, the results of this study suggest that partners are willing to discuss such issues and work them out, even if they involve infidelity.

Ideally, what is necessary is for partners to incorporate discussion of sexual matters and issues into the marital relational script such that it sustains throughout the lifespan of the relationship. Relationships evolve and infidelity is present in as many as one in four marriages (Wiederman, 1997). With the rise of HIV infection among heterosexuals through heterosexual sex, it is necessary for spouses to realize and personalize potential risks and engage in pertinent discussions.

ACKNOWLEDGEMENT

This chapter is based on a study conducted by Emmers-Sommer and Crowell (1999).

Homosexual Relationships and Safer Sex

If there is a success story about the response of any community to the awareness of HIV as a health risk, it is probably the adult gay male community. Shilts
(1987) in his book, *And the Band Played On*, documents the tentative and often
slow response by the adult gay male community to the growing threat of the
disease. The early response was tainted by a suspicious reaction to any public
health information or initiative viewed as inspired by a White House under
the Reagan administration viewed as hostile to gay interests. The feeling by
many in the gay community was that the White House and most of the administration as well as legislative branch (and for that matter much of society)
had not only abandoned interest in the gay community but became actively
hostile as the media and others began to speak about the "gay plague" or use
the term "GRID" (gay related infectious disease). The result was an unwillingness to react to what was a perceived growing public health crisis. This paraly-
sis, founded on fear and suspicion of governmental agencies created a delay in
the response of social communities to a medical condition. Even after HIV,
the outbreak of SARS found the People's Republic of China unable or unwilling to handle the fundamental issues of dealing with a contagious disease.

The term *plague* is particularly an issue given that the term invokes an old
Biblical term of what Moses inflicted on the Pharaoh of Egypt for refusing to
change his behavior to what God had proscribed. In the 1980s, cities and states
were expressing a more tolerant, if not encouraging, attitude towards homosexuals in society, going so far as to include "domestic partner unions" and re-
moving many of the legal and other restrictions. However, such actions need
to be counterbalanced against decisions by courts, like the Supreme Court in
Bowers v. Hardwick (1986). This Supreme Court decision found that state laws
that made private homosexual conduct between consenting adults illegal
were legitimate expressions of social moral codes. The court reasoned that

given all laws are founded on some moral principle, the generation of behavioral restrictions is permitted and only limited on the basis of prohibitions found in the constitution. Given sexual behavior is not constitutionally protected according to the court, the legislature can make such conduct illegal. The impact is the legitimization of state legislatures choosing to enact restrictions on sexual actions, even those occurring privately and between consenting adults on the basis of moral objection. Fundamentalist Christians can find moral objections to homosexuality in Biblical passages that become a basis for finding God's plan in HIV infection. The evidence of the "wages of sin" for the transgression of moral law found in God's word becomes rooted in the HIV epidemic. The problem from a public health perspective is finding a mechanism to deal the circumstances of what is perceived as God's just retribution for violation of natural law. The result is a disinclination for the population to undertake policies or provide for persons whose behavior is considered immoral and therefore illegal.

The social code issues become manifested in terms of homophobia. Homophobia presents an unreasoned fear of homosexuals and homosexuality. The problem that HIV provided was that it gave heterosexuals a basis for that fear. One of the authors was a debate coach in the early 1980s and there was a discussion among the staff about what to do with a homosexual on the team that was very "out." At the time, articles about GRID and the issues of a "gay cancer" that was spread by unknown means. The discussion centered on whether to take any action with a very sexually active young male and the danger of the disease. Debate travel often involves overnight lodging in shared rooms and extended periods confined in a van during travel. The thought of someone with an unknown and deadly disease in close contact for a long period of time created some nervousness.

Eventually, the consensus reached was that if the disease was related to homosexual behavior then heterosexuals were safe. If the disease was as contagious as the common cold, we were probably already infected. Obviously, we permitted the gay male to remain a member of the team and maintain normal travel patterns. At times the author has wondered the extent to which the resolution we reached, while justified, was based on a discussion that came from some type of fear of the sexuality of another person. The problem was that public health issues were raised about members of a group that seemed to share something in common. The nexus of what that commonality implied for the disease was never fully established, only the connection to the disease. Consider that for many individuals, the minimal fear of homosexuality to begin with searches for a justification for that fear. HIV provided a justification for that fear, even after the disease was clearly related to heterosexual behavior as well. The results, however, of the original and continuing stigma of the disease on a single part of the population plays an important and continual role in keeping homosexual males closeted away from the eyes of the larger general community.

The results of the manifestation of moral code as expressed in legal restrictions creates a community whose behavior is always viewed outside the law and social boundaries. The impact of the social regulation creates a community that exists outside of the general popular culture with a set of social norms developed by the community and generally known only to members of that community. The popular culture manifestations of gay society are often expressed through ambiguity, double meanings, or by artists already considered outside of the norm or on the fringe. The impact of this practice is the creation and use of stereotypes by the media. The manifestations of these stereotypes are the development by the majority that there exists a hidden community with different meanings and behaviors. This hidden community represents practices that are considered both immoral and illegal. In particularly conservative communities, the impact is the closeting of sexual practices behind doors and symbols that escape most of the rest of the community. In the more open and diverse communities, the symbols may still exist but the markings of membership in various communities are not nearly as hidden or ambiguous.

This questionable legal status of gay sexual relationships means that the community is functioning often in the context of clear moral as well as legal objections to the conduct of many members. The development of social scripts becomes not only a means for regulating behavior but provides some additional benefits by creating symbols and meanings only shared by members of the community and outside of the mainstream. With gay men the diversity of sexual preferences and behaviors finds a far wider scope of permissible and expected behaviors than most heterosexual communities. For most heterosexuals the development of trust within a relationship permits more diverse sexual practices. For many homosexual males the relationship is often more immediately sexual and gratification for the individual a higher priority. This means that the sexual encounter is more likely to be negotiated in the beginning with respect to the types of sexual behavior expected and the roles of the individuals in performing those behaviors. This expectation for general sexual practices means the gay males are more likely to find explicit and detailed sexual discussions with potential partners more acceptable and therefore more comfortable than most heterosexual couples.

However, by the early 1990s, condom use and the issue of safer sex as well as information about testing and treatment were dominant topics of the gay community. Probably no other issue more deeply affected a group than the recognition of the risk of the disease for the sexually active gay male. The response by members of the community was overwhelming as changes in the entire set of sexual behaviors occurred in order to diminish the risk of infection. The issues of how to generate an appropriate and effective response to any community requires an understanding of the social and cultural specificity (Croteau, Nero, & Prosser, 1993). What this change amounted to was the introduction of an innovation designed to improve the public health of the community (Rogers, 1995; Rogers & Shefner-Rogers, 1999).

The gay male community's sexual practices permitted persons to engage in unprotected sex with a large number of partners in a relatively short time period. Given the higher rate of HIV transmission for anal sex, the potential for the spread of the virus was higher than other communities (with the exception of those receiving blood transfusions, hemophiliacs, or intravenous drug users sharing needles). Members of the gay male community engaging in unprotected anal sex with multiple sex partners created the conditions for rapid transmission in the community. The community was identifiable and often members were known to each other. The "secret" community had ways of gathering and communicating with each other through various social networks that while not totally invisible were often outside the mainstream of society. But the symbols were apparent to most of the members of the group.

Gagnon and Simon (1973) point out that sexual behavior becomes significant when a collective life defines the behavior or view as significant. For the gay male, the acceptance of a sexual preference, "I am gay," represents a coming out, that when acknowledged and reinforced by others becomes something significant. Gay males typically define themselves as homosexual and the acceptance of that behavior becomes significant to other gay men as well as to the rest of society. To generate or to operate within the community involves the acceptance of various rituals and markers that create the definition of the gay man. As Simon and Gagnon (1986) point out that the social significance of these changes, "sociogenic" must also create an individual experience or development that assigns significance for the individual person, "ontogenic."

The question was whether the community (sociogenic) would respond to the request for a modification in behavior of individuals (ontogenic). The request had to come from governmental sources associated with the medical community. The perceived antipathy of the government in the 1980s (during the Reagan administration) to issues that effected gay males created a fundamental set of barriers to generated effective and immediate community response and endorsement of necessary steps to diminish the risk of transmission. The role of social support for behavioral change plays an important part because if everyone is making the change together than the acceptance for self (ontogenic) is consistent with acceptance of the collective (sociogenic).

What this implies is that a successful change involves not only individual acceptance of the need for change, but the acceptance of the larger social system of the need for such a change. The question of who is asking for the change or expects the change is not an unimportant question. When the advice for the change comes external to the community, the basis for the reasons that the agent is asking for the change becomes subject to scrutiny. The fundamental change for the gay male community involves a change in sexual practices and the ultimate performance of the behaviors will require internal acceptance (if not outright endorsement) of the changes by the community.

The translation must go from belief to behavioral intentions and then to action. The reinforcement of the beliefs and behaviors becomes a community belief and the social more that subscribes to that belief and practice. The theory of reasoned action (Fishbein & Ajzen, 1985) continues to receive attention as a basis for understanding the translation of attitude to behavior. Hale, Householder, and Greene (2003) document the numerous meta-analyses (Ajzen, 1991; Godin & Kok, 1996; Hausenblas, Carron, & Mack, 1997; Kim & Hunter, 1993a, 1993b: Randall & Wolff, 1994; Sheeran & Oberall, 1998; Sheeran & Taylor, 1999; Sheppard, Hartwick, & Warshaw, 1988).

TIME TO CHANGE THE SCRIPT

Like with most uses of scripts, the development of scripts or routinized behavior can be problematic if the pattern turns out to promote risk of any negative or antisocial outcome. The carefree days of anonymous and promiscuous sexual encounters without concern about the spread of a fatal and incurable disease ended rather abruptly. The developed script for sexual encounters required revision in response to the threat of a communicable disease. Simon and Gagnon (1986) point out the sexual scripts, although developed through adolescence, are subject to change over the life cycle. The problem is that the motivation or mechanism for change must find a basis to provide reasons or opportunities for modification in behavior.

Probably no example illustrates the issues more completely than what the CDC termed "patient zero." Shilts (1987) points out that this was a French Canadian man considered extremely attractive and an airline steward. He was traveling around the country and enjoyed going to bathhouses in major cities and having sex with large numbers of men. The impact of his having been infected early was that he infected a large number of men. The fundamental issue was that originally he would be able to have unprotected sex with large numbers of willing, even eager partners, however, as the knowledge of the disease began to become known, the reaction to anyone, even the most beautiful and available began to change.

The community began to adopt different sexual mores and more and more gay males began to diminish the level of risk behaviors in their lives. McCoy and Inciardi (1995) detail some of the changes or at least the increased awareness that grew in the gay community about the need for safer sexual practices.

These changes occurred all over the Western World as the sexually active gay men began to react and reduce risk (Christiansen & Lowhagen, 2000). A big set of changes was the adoption of safer sex (mostly the use of a condom during anal sex) for sex with secondary or tertiary partners. Many men would have unprotected anal sex with their main partners (Elford, Bolding, Maguire, & Sherr, 1999). This behavior is safe only if the partners are seroconcordant and negative. The problem is that 50% of men were not aware of their own HIV status, their partner's or both (Elford, Bolding, Maguire, & Sherr, 1999). The impact of HIV was to develop a kind of negotiated safety where a male couple would create a sense of commitment to only have unprotected sex with a single partner in a relationship (Kippax, Crawford, Davis, Rodden, & Dowsett, 1993; Kippax et al., 1997). But this commitment only creates a sexual safety zone if both partners are aware of their HIV status and practice a monogamous sexual relationship. The difficulty of the community maintaining fidelity to that view represents a fundamental problem in handling the HIV epidemic.

The goal of HIV prevention programs is ultimately the adoption of behavior by a target group that reduces risk of infection. The ultimate goal remains the development of routinized behavior such that a gay male about to engage in sex will either have sexual behavior with lower risk (e.g., mutual manual masturbation) or use methods that decrease the potential for infection (wearing a condom during sex). The goal of having just a set of routinized behaviors for engaging in sex would diminish the risk.

For example, most Americans when they get into a car have the habit of wearing a seatbelt; the habit, developed over the years becomes so routine that the person may not be actively engaged in thinking about the need to perform the behavior but simply does it because the script of riding in a motor vehicle expects are requires that particular action. The goal for educational interventions was the development of the same attitude toward a person about the engage in sex. The challenge was to create a set of materials and conditions that would promote persons to practice safer sexual behaviors.

One of the authors was conducting some interviews with gay men in bars about sexual behavior. The places commonly had bowls of condoms on the tables and typically some type of information about HIV infection was placed on tables or on the walls in the bathrooms. The message was communicated loudly and clearly that not only was the establishment concerned with the sexual behavior of the customers, but that a particular sexual behavior was encouraged. Many of the gay men felt that routinely they would insist that all anal sex involve the use of a condom (however, many admitted that if the partner was really good looking and insistent, they might not make that a firm requirement).

Consider that by contrast, very few, if any, heterosexual bars (even those designated as "meat markets") would distribute and display condoms on the table. This difference begins to illustrate how the nature of the differences in scripts between the gay male and heterosexual communities manifests not only in a conversational distinction but behaviorally as well. But this distinction on the basis of condom visibility and use was not always the case; the growth in the use and acceptability (and for some time the preference) for condom use was not always taken for granted.

Conversation (gossiping) about sexual practices was common in social settings, the conversations included those persons "safe" and those persons at risk. Also, gossip about those persons that were "sick" and various information about new treatments and possibilities for dealing with HIV/AIDS was not an infrequent source of conversation. In some ways, it was a relatively important and for some an almost obsessive source of conversation. The focus on relationships received a lot of attention because the knowledge that sexual practices that involved the collaboration with a safe steady partner created a primary focus on relationships.

The community took notice of the dead and those that were dying as well as rumors about treatments, vaccines, and potential cures. The community had come together over an issue of immense importance. The fact that the larger community of heterosexuals and most of the official governmental agencies and new organizations did little to publicize or explore the events contributed to the development of social networks of information. The development of the web pages provided the means for many persons to communicate over distance and time to others about topics of mutual importance.

The level of consciousness about the issues provided a focal point that required members of the culture to begin to deal with the fundamental issues. The discussion about condoms however did not fundamentally change the approach of the community to sexual discussions. Discussions about sexuality were a primary source of conversation and attention by the community, what changed was the content of the discussion. The conversation essentially expanded to simply include another consideration or event in the process.

The adult gay male community therefore already had the mechanism to permit the discussion of safer sex into the community. At the same time, the recognition of interaction with the persons living with HIV created an explicit awareness of the disease (see collection by Derlega & Barbee, 1998). Collins (1998) reports that gay men report often the existence of social support and a sense of solidarity within the gay community after contracting the disease. This however should be contrasted with reports of African-American gay men that find themselves identifying with the African-American community more than the gay community (Icard, 1986; Johnson, 1987; Rose, 1998).

DOUBLE EDGED SWORD

The problem starting at the turn of the century was the effectiveness of various therapies, including the drug cocktail. The problem with the effectiveness of any treatment is the reduction in the associated fear of the corresponding disease. The less the fear, the reduced ability of messages designed to reduce risk behaviors. This is of concern, particularly for young gay males. As mentioned, although safer sex practices have been embraced by much of the older, adult gay male community, safer sex practices are seemingly abandoned by many young, gay, and bisexual males. This adandonment is largely attributed to the young, gay males' reliance on drug cocktails if need be (CDC, 2002). A primary consideration in health campaign messages is the fear of the consequences for failure to adopt a particular behavioral routine (Witte & Allen, 2000).

The sexual transformation is always generational. The older generation of gay males lost friends, family, and lovers to the conditions caused by HIV. However, among the younger set of gay males, fewer of them have direct experience with persons dying horrible deaths because of HIV infection. This lack of personal experience means that the level of immediate fear and concern for the disease has less sense of immediacy and vulnerability.

The disease, or more precisely, the fear of the disease becomes something for the elderly (in this case over 30). What happens is that perception of the disease begins to become something related to age as the fear of the disease diminishes with more effective treatment, community values and mores begin to erode. If the premise driving the actions of safer sex are no longer as strong a motivating influence, then the solidarity of the community no longer is evident and behavior reverts to something more natural and appealing.

THE CHALLENGE OF BAREBACKING

The introduction of "barebacking" as a means of sexual practice by gay men produced a unique set of risks. Barebacking comes from the rodeo designation where the cowboy rides a horse or bull without a saddle. Applied to sexual practices, barebacking meant sex without use of condoms. The nonuse of the condom was associated with some sexual thrill seeking and extended the sense of anonymity practiced in some of the bathhouses.

Barebacking parties or clubs became a practice where use of condoms, questioning a partner about previous sexual practices, or any other kind of risk reduction was considered inappropriate. The behavioral routine, depending on the content, can provide an increased risk for a person engaging in behaviors that increase the risk of infection. The goal of the encounter is sexual interaction with another person based on minimal information being exchanged.

The sexual script for these encounters implied anonymous and consensual anal sex without the use of a condom. The implication was that each person assumed the risk and made no promises or statements about HIV status or sexual history.

The script for these encounters requires a bit of understanding on the part of the participants about how sexual encounters will be managed.

The net result of the barebacking practices is a high-risk sexual conduct. The participation in these endeavors is a form of Russian roulette or taking a dare with the sexuality. A couple of participants in these encounters have told one of the authors that the risks and possible outcomes are understood, but that risk simply adds to the thrill of the experience and the uncertainty of the outcomes associated with engaging in anonymous sex with an unknown partner. The very risk of infection and possibility of illness adds to the sensation of the event. Taking a risk on a sexual encounter becomes a part of the experience.

The issues of the bathhouse represent as Elwood and Williams (1999) point out, "politics of silence." What happens is that the persons involved in sexual decision making have to decide whether or not to engage in safe sex. But the issue is one conducted in silence, the act of conversation or discussion is not something sanctioned, in fact, talking is considered inappropriate. Consider, that for heterosexuals, the act of conversation increases the probability of condom use (see meta-analysis, Allen et al., 2002, $r = .156$). The failure to incorporate a conversational element in the sexual act, particularly given the conditions of the bathhouse, may reduce the probability of condom use.

Part of the decision is that the norm has been established that the "top" person assumes the dominant role and determines whether or not the sex will involve a condom use. This role is consistent with Hispanic males that have sex with men who only define the "bottom" role as homosexual or effeminate (Bradford, Allen, Casey, & Emmers-Sommer, 2002). This "bottom" role is referred to in the homosexual literature as "bottom shame."

The term *barebacking* has evolved in usage to indicate a much wider use. The term now is sometimes used to indicate a person that "forgot" to use a condom. Barebacking has gone from a rather specialized event to a more general description of a term. The question for behavioral scientists is what kinds of circumstances or changes in conditions have increased the acceptability of this practice.

DIFFERENCE IN AGE, DIFFERENCES IN ATTITUDE

Interview a set of older (over 30 years old) gay men and most of them are very anxious about HIV infection. Most of them grew up during the scare and the knowledge of thousands of persons dying due to AIDS related conditions. Such personal involvement with persons infected with HIV, particularly during the early stages of the epidemic created a fundamental crisis and personal effect of the disease. The disease was not an academic or exercise in a distant and impersonal kind of experience. The direct experience of something that was unknown and uncertain creates an entire generation of gay men that confronted a potentially terrifying future as well as the potential of the entire stigma of a disease affixed to their identity.

Interviews demonstrate a kind of fear about sexual encounters and the risk of HIV infection that is often not a present in the younger crowd. The current generation of young gay men (in their early 20s) have never known an environment without the risk of HIV. The cultural revolution that Shilts (1987) described of sexual freedom is simply not known by the young gay male community. Safer sex requirements for condom use serves as a backdrop to sexual activity for this generation.

Although that risk is apparent, the increased effectiveness of treatment has also meant a diminished fear of the disease (Allen et al., 2002; Gagnon & Godin, 2000). The current generation has less sense of risk and personal loss from knowing members of the community that were lost due to the epidemic.

The paradox for the community becomes the issues of higher levels of knowledge about the disease exists. HIV and AIDS are topics of general and real concern to the community. The individuals in the community spend a great deal of time working on issues relating to education and prevention. The knowledge about treatment is also higher than the general population. However, as treatments become more effective, the level of fear about the disease diminishes. Consider that most Americans seldom boil drinking water or worry about the quality of the water coming from a tap. But outbreaks of various diseases have occurred when the purification system did not work.

The younger generation has also seen the rise of the AIDS denialists, groups of individuals that deny that HIV infection causes AIDS. The group argues against safe sex, testing for HIV, and the participation on various treatments for HIV. The argument is that the scientific community has misidentified the cause of AIDS and is ultimately discriminating against members of the community. The group also argues that it is the treatments for HIV infection that are more likely to kill a person.

THE CHALLENGE OF DRUG USE

Issues involving the use of drugs and sexual behavior are nothing new; the discovery of alcohol probably goes back to antiquity and the relationship to sexual behavior. What is important for this discussion is that sexual behavior while under the influence of various substances diminishes the use of condoms, particularly for gay men. The implementation of a script for behavior while under the influence remains a great barrier for safer sexual behavior in any population.

The best plans of the individual to use a condom can easily fall apart if the person is either drunk or using some other substance that distorts the judgment of the person. The use of drugs when considerations about sexual behavior are involved represents a diminished capacity for reasoned judgment and adherence to developed behavioral intentions. Essentially, drug use in clubs or at parties, places where sexual behavior is negotiated or inspired represents setting least likely to find support for safer sexual practices. Because most of these settings are likely to involve sexual practices with causal partners, the result is the kind of sexual encounter that is more likely to involve the potential for risk.

The acceptability, if not endorsement, of casual sexual relations between persons in the gay community means that drugs diminishes the lack of reasoning and critical judgment in all matters. When deciding to have sex with another man, the influence of drugs probably increases the availability of the other person and diminishes the behavioral routines that a person generally has developed for sexual encounters. The person must make choices, particularly if the other person is resisting the desire to use a condom.

The development of social scripts generally assumes the ability and / or willingness to implement the scripts. The use of drugs represents a loss of cognitive functioning that reduces condom use (Hingson, Strunin, Berlin, & Heeren,

1990; Perry et al., 1994). The loss of reasoning and of the fear of the disease may make the use of drugs something that contributes to increased risk.

Given the high use of drugs (particularly alcohol) in the gay community, the good intentions of the individual may simply not be implemented in the heat of passion. What this indicates is a conflict in the desire of the person between passionate experiences (often defined as heat of the moment or spontaneous) and the requirements of planning and forethought (seen as antithetical to the views of passionate love). The problem represents an interesting dilemma, especially for a community of persons whose credo often involves the freedom of casual sexual encounters without fear of pregnancy or other commitment. The expectation of a life of relative sexual freedom from the rejection of most social mores becomes then constrained by the imposition of requirements for "safety" and health considerations.

The problem is that "forgetting" or "making an exception" becomes represents an acceptable or permissible excuse within the community. The mistake caused by alcohol or other drugs begins to play a part in the decision to take risks. The decision to take a risk is not seen as having the same consequences for the participant and decisions must be made. The fundamental impact of this view is a weakening or a decline in the seriousness of the commitment to safer sexual practices. The script becomes more conditional and subject to circumstances rather than representing a universal set of expectations for all sexual encounters.

Sexual risk implies a shared activity (given masturbation would involve no risk). If both persons share the same attitude and behavior toward using a condom then the risk is managed (either a condom is used to diminish risk or not used). However, when the desires of the persons are discordant and one person desires to use a condom and the other person does not, the process requires some type of negotiation or agreement that permits the sexual actions to proceed (assuming that one person simply does not use force or coercion to have the other person submit).

One change is that the fear of the spread of the disease has moved on from this community to now minority women. Increasingly, gay male groups find themselves in competition for prevention money for condoms and educational materials with other groups now considered more at risk.

CONCLUSION

The gay male community, like most cultural groups is really not a single group. The community has the AIDS denialists, those persons that deny a link between HIV infection and subsequent development of AIDS and opportunistic infection. Similarly, heterosexuals (like Maggiore) deny the existence of the disease or would deny the important of the disease (Fumento, 1988). However, the broad community generally recognizes the existence and danger of HIV infection. Even if not fatal, the diminution in the quality of life and the long-term health implications (without a cure, vaccine, or effective treatment, very negative prognosis) for contracting the virus. The consequences of testing positive for HIV represent not only a health issue for the individual, but an additional health issue for the rest of society (a sexually active person with the virus can infect others). The critical need is to prevent the spread of the disease among those at risk for contracting the disease. The older generation of gay males responded to the existence of the threat by coming together to change sexual practices. The collective did not impose formal sanctions on deviant members, each gay male was free to practice sexuality consistent with beliefs, but risky sex is a shared activity and each person can decide what level of risk to accept in a particular sexual encounter. A vast majority of gay men chose to reduce the risk of exposure to infection and the spread of the disease slowed.

The question is now the second generation of gay males dealing with this viral infection. The first generation of gay men went through a kind of culture shock as many persons died around the community as the disease spread silently and almost unnoticed, without a name, until the disease was an epidemic.

The need to manage or handle sexual interaction, in the various guises and locations, has generated sequences of behavior that permit a negotiation of interaction. The generation of scripts or sequences of behavior becomes a marker of various attitudes held about HIV infection and the need or desire for safer sex. Given that the gay community was largely and immediately impacted on by the spread of HIV in the 1980s, it is difficult to find a gay male from that time that does not know someone that died from the disease. The connection or experience with the disease is personal and immediate, and the need for protection viewed as essential.

The problem faced by the gay male community is the lack of mainstream or general acceptance by the larger community. The very kind of outsider, marginal, or fringe sense of the community can feed the desire and justification to reject conventional advice. The advice of the medical or public health community becomes rejected as part of the majority's attempt to control the community. Rejection of this suggestion for behavior represents a reaffirmation of the liberation of the community from conventional and oppressive morality.

The conversations in the community continue to go on. Social scripts function within the popular as accepted cultural norms. The community of gay males grew in solidarity and awareness as a result of the tragedy of HIV / AIDS in the 1980s and 1990s. The community survived in part, because the commu-

nity adapted the sexual practices reflected in the expected script for sexual conduct. The unique openness to the discussion of explicit sexual behavior makes
change possible. Whether other such communities exist or the possibility of
developing such an attitude seems rather difficult.

However, the dynamics of creating a culture or having a cultural response
to external pressures presents the gay male community as an interesting and
important example of a response to a health crisis that can be affected through
behavioral change. The impact of HIV is not simply a public health issue; HIV
represents an issue of social and cultural practices.

The gay male community represents the paradox of an informed community reacting quickly to the threat. The sexual script changed as the collective
society began to define significance to the event and the safer sexual behaviors. The acceptance of this change represents individuals accepting the need
for a change that becomes reinforced by members of the society sharing and
similarly accepting the behavior as part of the sexual script.

The continuity of the change, or a continued commitment to the maintenance of the script, remains challenging and a fundamental problem. The initial considerations that led to the rise of the change in the sexual practices has
begun to fade in the presence of newer therapies and a new generation that
has accepted and lived with the fear of the disease from the beginning. But the
new generation of young gay males has not had the same experiences of
watching members of the community die from terrible and tragic diseases on
a daily basis. The deaths now are much more prolonged and members of the
community have begun to argue from the denialist standpoint. The unity or
the coherence necessary to maintain the script of safer sexual behaviors may
be impossible to continue.

Culture and Safer Sex Behaviors

The issues involved in sexuality are important in defining the individual, and the relationships with others. But the sexual practices of the individual occur within a culture context that supports and defines the practices. Many cultures would view sexual practices as an inherent and important part of any definition of the identity of the person. This chapter considers the issues of sexuality and culture as those considerations play a role in the understanding of HIV education and prevention efforts. The development of a script for sexual interaction reflects not only personal desires and values but must take place within a cultural setting (Metts & Spitzberg, 1996; Whittier & Simon, 2001). The appropriateness of various behaviors and the understood or believed suitability of various actions must be contained within a cultural framework that permits persons to understand and manage human interaction. This chapter provides a consideration of alternative ethnic groups and the importance that culture, as measured by ethnic origins, plays in dealing with HIV education and prevention.

This chapter considers the intersection of what amounts to scripts or issues dealing with sequences or expectations of behavior and the definition or practices of a culture. Sequences or expectations arise from issues imbedded or imparted by a sense of cultural identity. The defining elements of identity may involves the enactment of such rituals with specified practices to reinforce fundamental values of the culture as well as create a shared identity. Given the importance of sexuality to individuals and the stress placed on sexuality within the United States, all individuals, regardless of initial cultural position, face decisions about behavior that reflect important identity considerations. What constitutes coercive or inappropriate sexual actions become evaluated within the context of the values for sexual actions (Burt, 1980; Emmers-Sommer & Allen, 1999). Culture serves the basis of identification and knowing or believing that the behavior engaged in is appropriate.

DEFINING CULTURE

We define culture as a community of persons that share a common set of symbols. The term *language community* best describes the approach that represents the broad view we have of the issues of culture. A culture is a collection of people that share a common set of experiences and views that are expressed through a common shared symbol system. Every culture has references or vocabulary that a member of that culture is expected to know.

A person can belong to multiple cultures at the same time. Cultural groups are not exclusive; language use and symbol sharing are common among groups. However, the meaning or importance of particular terms or symbols may differ significantly for each group. The groups can be based on some shared value, common set of experiences, as well as ethnic and racial designations. The distance between generations (parent and child) often represent distances between cultures where symbols (slang, clothing, music, etc.) become cultural artifacts and representations for a generation that provides a sense of symbolic unity. The critical feature is whether the use and maintenance of the symbols creates a sense of unity or shared identity apart from other identities that others may have. Consider that in terms of HIV risk, there exist the communities of the intravenous drug user, the commercial sex worker, and so on, and each carries a unique set of risk and uncertainties with regard to HIV infection. The fundamental question is whether a male sex worker having sex with other men should be considered part of the homosexual community or the commercial sex worker community when addressing the nature of the risk. Such assignments may require the consideration of the multiple nature of the communities to which one belongs. Consider that for some persons in larger cities that are "hustling" to provide resources, such persons do not necessarily see themselves as either gay or as a commercial sex worker but may be involved in behaviors that resemble risks of both groups. If the person is African American, then the issues are compounded and confused. The sexual or HIV risk scripts involved should be considered and how the practices modified to reduce risk needs to be considered as well.

Groups can contain subgroups that would appear to share relatively few symbols but more symbols ore shared references that larger groups. The question is whether a person shares what level of primary sense of identification with which particular group. The identification serves as the basis of deciding which set of social scripts to enact and the appropriateness of enacting particular sequences of behavior. The person must make judgments about what sets of behaviors are appropriate for the setting and the others involved. Given the types of conflict in identity that may exist for an individual, the ability to define and recognize the situation may contribute to the enactment of a particular script.

This chapter considers four groups in the United States: (1) Hispanic or La-tino, (2) African American, (3) Native American, and (4) Asian American. Each group represents a set of cultural communities with varying degrees of risk for HIV infection. The coming challenge of HIV education and prevention is the identification and application of behavioral interventions that must be adapted to the needs and requirements of particular groups. The application of general interventions predicated on the needs of the majority or main-stream will prove ineffective in application or even exposure to various groups whose media, education, and other sources and evaluations of con-tacts differ from the mainstream.

A central issue is that these groups represent racial or ethnic groups that contain many different subgroups. The representation in this chapter is sim-ply a consideration of general issues that are thought to be common to many members of that particular culture. This represents the process of oversim-plification and generates a certain mismatch between the representation of the culture and the target of the various messages. However, such a mis-match is inevitable and unavoidable. Given the alternatives of either endless reduction of information to particular communities and subcommunities or the ignoring of the communities and the treatment of a supra or metaculture that exists that transcends the individuality of various communities, we pre-fer to take a midrange approach that will do some violence and ignore partic-ular small communities but does not simply claim that there exists one common "American" culture.

THE IMPORTANCE OF IDENTITY FOR THE INDIVIDUAL

An important part of a person's identity comes from the sense of affect held about the ethnic or racial group of which a person considers themselves a part. Sexual identity is only one part of a person's sense of identity but the general features of a person's identity are not unimportant. The importance of sexual-ity identity and the adoption or endorsement of various scripts for behavior plays an important role in the development of the person.

A person develops a self-image based on a number of factors. Typically, persons in the quantitative literature have taken self-image or self esteem and divided that into three different components, particularly for children and ad-olescents. The importance of racial group orientation to self-concept has been demonstrated in a an existing meta-analysis (Allen, Howard, & Grimes, 1997). The overall correlation across 38 studies involving 8,475 participants was .14, which indicates a 33% increase in self-concept associated with above average levels of a positive feeling about one's own racial group (using the Binomial Effect Size Display [BESD], Rosenthal, 1984).

The failure to maintain a positive identity is associated with various anti-social outcomes including educational failure, use of substances, and criminal activity. The important of handling the pressures and issues of sexuality must come from within the acceptance and understanding as well as the development of particular scripts for behavior.

HISPANIC CULTURAL ISSUES

The term *Hispanic* represents a class lot of terms (Latino, South American, Caribbean, etc.) to refer to a group of persons that are descendents from persons in Central or South America (including the Caribbean). Other terms have and continue to be used as this loose group of persons seeks to create a sense of identity that reflects both shared and different characteristics. Part of the problem in dealing with this particular class of individuals is that an Hispanic will often also be a national of a variety of different countries (e.g., Mexico, Guatemala, Venezuela, Peru, Chile, etc.). The person will have differences and distinctions from other Hispanics based on the nation of origin. Many Hispanics are often persons with mixed native and European origins and therefore may differ on the basis of religion and ethnic practices. At the same time, not all persons living in South America or the Caribbean would consider themselves members of Hispanic culture. The result is that a person entering the United States may be classified or thought of as Hispanic and within that particular cultural group may represent a large amount of diversity along a variety of different dimensions.

The sources of information for this group may involve less traditional mechanisms used when compared to the majority population in the United States.

A central issue dealing with Hispanic culture dealing with sexuality is machismo (MacLachlan, 1997). This identification with a particular set of aggressive needs by males to achieve a sense of power and domination influences a number of sexual practices. Machismo becomes related to a strong need to fulfill social demands or expectation for male dealing with highly ritualized and identified sex roles. A particular part of the role of the male in classic Hispanic culture requires a great deal of control or domination, particularly of a wife or a girlfriend. A female should be a virgin until marriage and remain faithful to the husband. Females often develop scripts to handle unwanted sexual advances (Frith & Kitzinger, 2001). The husband operates in a system that espouses marital fidelity (both as a cultural and a religious value) but recognizes and to some extent permits sexual infidelity. Generally, the script for behavior permits sexuality and sexual practices to be more than likely dominated by the man. Virginity is often thought of as abstaining from vaginal sex.

One outcome of this sexual role identification is a male that has sex with other men. The problem is how Latino males find a way to engage in sex with other males and maintain a masculine identity that does not create a homosexual identity.

The Hispanic Émigré

The person arriving in the United States from a Latino country (Cuba, Nicaragua, Bolivia, El Salvador, Mexico, etc.,) leaves one culture (the one from the geographic location of origin) and enters a new culture. The person arriving in the United States probably wants to adapt and acculturate by changing practices to become part of the new culture. At a minimum, the person leaves a culture dominated probably by persons speaking Spanish and enters a culture where the dominant language is English (or American) and where Spanish may or may not be spoken by many persons in the same location. Not surprisingly, many persons arriving will seek out parts of the community where persons sharing similar cultural and language backgrounds exist.

Operationally, most measures of acculturation reflect the issues related to use of language (Marin, Sabogal, Marin, Otero-Sabogal, & Perez-Stable, 1987).

Distinguishing Types of Relationships

Doval, Duran, O'Donnell, and O'Donnell (1995) report that Hispanic STD clinic attendees distinguish between primary and secondary relationships. Condom use was *not* prevalent with persons that were considered primary sexual partners. However, condom use increased dramatically with sexual partners that were not considered part of a primary relationship. The issue is an important one because it indicates that issues of trust and concern do exist but are differentiated on the basis of the relationship. This indicates that improved effectiveness for HIV education and interventions may need to recognize the distinction in this cultural group based not on the behavior involved but instead on the markers or definition of that relationship.

This educational message could be particularly effective because it serves to reinforce the existing sense of classification for sexual partners that currently exists. The message becomes one of identifying and classifying the existing relationships along a system currently in use. The script for safer sexual behavior would, if anything, serve to reinforce the existing social behavioral norm.

Why There are no Homosexual Hispanic Males

Latino culture produces a stance of males that represents a relatively high homophobia (Carillo & Urgaga-McKane, 1994). Due to machismo, Latino men may have sex with men but maintain rigid role differentiation. The man will usually take the role of either the male or female in penetration. In contrast to males in other cultures, Latino men rarely switch roles or engage in both roles. Males adopting the male penetration role frequently continue to classify themselves as heterosexual and engage in heterosexual relationships as well. The Latino reference to homosexuality usually involves a reference to the male that plays the female role in penetration. Men, acting the part of the female role are typically seen as effeminate, and derogated as men. Therefore, the reference MSM (men who have sex with men) is particularly appropriate because the reference points to the behavior that a person engaged in rather than some implied commentary on the "lifestyle" or "preference."

This particular social script that is used to classify a person as heterosexual means that targeting the "gay" community becomes ineffective. Education toward the "gay" male in the Hispanic community would mostly target the anal receptive member of the sexual dyad rather than the anal insertive member. The need to target effective education about condoms must apply to the insertive partner given the condom is worn by that male. Even if the anal receptive male receives the message, the "female" role is one of less power and the ability to assert the need to wear a condom may not be possible.

However, the construction of a message that differentiates between primary and secondary sexual partners might be effective. In this case, the educational materials target a naturally occurring category that capitalizes on the perspective of the actor's sexual orientation toward a primary partner (wife, fiancée, girlfriend) and then classifies other sexual encounters as secondary and therefore in need of protection. This particular script or classification is particularly salient because the secondary partner is considered to lack the same virtue or value (chastity) as the main or primary partner.

The feminization of the disease would particularly be effective because it would be the outcome of an action that would be targeted as undesirable.

AFRICAN AMERCIAN CULTURAL ISSUES

Probably no group is considered currently a higher risk for HIV infection than African American women. A central question is why is this particular group has greater infection rates than other groups. The particular concern is among African American women as a group, this particular group has among the highest infection rates. The focus is on understanding why this particular group has higher risk and what modifications are necessary in any education and prevention program. The perception that HIV infection and AIDS is a white gay male disease operates as a fundamental barrier to the development of sexual scripts rising out of concern of infection. If infection is not a primary fear, then the probability of any group adopting behaviors to reduce risk remains unlikely.

An upcoming book by J. L. King (2004) entitled, "On the Down Low" describes African-American men who are married or dating women but who also secretly have sex with men. This phenomenon is described by King as having sex on the "down low." King, himself, was married 8 years and often had sex with men surreptitiously. According to a report by Micah Materre on WGN News Chicago (2004), many African American men will not describe themselves as "gay," but might answer "yes" if asked if they have sex with other men. The report indicates that King went public with his lifestyle and the prevalence of the lifestyle in response to the rapid rise of HIV and AIDS among the African American community. Materre's report indicates that although African Americans are 12% of the United States population, they involve 50% of the HIV and AIDS cases. The report goes on to indicate that 64% of the new cases are African American women, who are 20 times more likely to contract HIV than a White woman. This "undercover" lifestyle begs additional attention and examination and should prompt African American women to ask certain questions of their male partner and to take personal precautions.

Another very real issue is the poverty and lack of economic power of this particular group. A central question is the sense of empowerment faced by women. Do women feel empowered and assertive enough to insist that a sexual partner use a condom, given previous research that suggests that women are more likely to initiate condom use (Allen et al., 2002).

Several surveys have pointed out that African American women do not belief themselves to be at risk for HIV infection (Mays & Cochran, 1988; Shervington, 1993). Cummings, Battle, Barker, and Krasnovsky (1999) report that 64% of 79 African American women have not used a condom in the last 6 months, the primary reason was a belief in a monogamous relationship with a male that was not an intravenous drug user and therefore that put them at a low risk for HIV transmission.

Although not solely particular to African American families, another aspect is a social system that rewards multiple children by increasing the size of the support check to the family for additional children, particularly children without a father physically present. The social system creates a reward system associated with having multiple children, any social pressure to have children will diminish the desire for a person to engage in safer sexual behaviors. This is particularly relevant to condom use because the condom is not only a way to diminish sexually transmitted diseases but also functions as a means of contraception. HIV infection is related to the economic status of the community because of the reality of the desire for children, often associated with a lower income. The increased desire for children reduces the use of condoms because it interferes with another goal.

The problem of the sexual script in African American relationships comes from a lot of focus group and other considerations dealing with the cultural norms about parenthood and sexual behavior.

Earvin "Magic" Johnson's announcement that he was HIV positive created a temporary view that the disease was not that simply for White gay males. The impact of his announcement was to demonstrate to increase testing and knowledge (Casey et al., 2003).

NATIVE AMERICAN CULTURAL ISSUES

Native American populations demonstrate considerable risk, but relatively little behavioral information is collected on this particular group, compared to other ethnic minorities.

One focus group study involving Native Americans generated information concentrating on the nature of despair and hopelessness of the part of the participants. The frequent references to alcoholism and factors associated with poverty pointed to HIV risk factors as simply part of a lifestyle that is fraught with danger, disease, and a lack of hope.

Essentially, HIV risk is simply one risk in a panoply of possible negative health outcomes faced by this population. The threat of HIV infection simply does not create a unique or compelling threat. The fundamental emotional response listed in the one focus group investigation of Native-American populations was essentially despair (Baldwin, Trotter, Martinez, Stevens, John, & Brems, 1999). The despair came from viewing HIV infection as simply adding to a long list of current problems facing the community.

The focus of such messages must be ones dealing with the issues of both self-efficacy as well as the need to deal with response efficacy. Current research dealing with fear appeals (Witte & Allen, 2000) indicates that a fear appeal is more effective when both elements are present in a message. HIV education and prevention programs operate by providing information about a threat or concern that can be mitigated or reduced by the adoption of particular behaviors. The underlying assumption is that the group receiving the information has a minimum set of hopes or aspirations that would be denied by failure to adopt the necessary protective behaviors. A person must feel that the threat is serious and the individual is vulnerable to the threat. The purpose of the intervention is to reduce the negative consequences by providing a substitute. However, such messages are less effective if the population is not concerned about the threat because of other greater concerns.

ASIAN AMERICAN CULTURAL ISSUES

Asian Americans are similar to the issues faced by Hispanics in dealing with populations in the United States for some time and some populations recently emigrated into the United States from some country. However, most Asian cultures are far more collective than Latino cultures and that creates a need for additional levels or expectations of conformity to various cultural demands.

A big distinction is that the need for conformity to established rules of behavior has little to do with various religious expectations, but instead comes from deeply held cultural beliefs. A critical question is where sexual beliefs come from as well as information about sexual behaviors. The importance of understanding the means of transmission of sexual information requires additional attention.

Many cultures do not involve or permit public discussions of sexual behavior. The transmission of knowledge may involve peers or family members (often communication is mother to daughter about sexual issues). The requirements of an educational program may not involve communication simply to the general public but instead may require the targeting of particular individuals that serve as opinion leaders or means of transmission to the target individuals.

DISCUSSION OF CULTURE IN HIV EDUCATION
AND PREVENTION

Sexual actions are important to individuals for a variety of emotional, psychological, and personal reasons. A defining element of just about any person is the issue of sexual practice. But identity for an individual also considers the issues of cultural identity and how sexual practices and conformity or acceptance of sexual mores leads to identification and enactment of the cultural identity. Educational interventions need to find ways of accepting the definition of fundamental values and relationships and work within that construct to promote behaviors that will diminish risk. This shift requires an increased use of qualitative methods and projects that seek to define cultural practices of various groups. Attempts to alter fundamental cultural values and the subsequent implied behaviors of such groups probably will fail.

A central element of any understanding of sexually transmitted disease prevention (including HIV) requires an understanding of how sexual information is transmitted within the society. Do members of a particular culture expect information to be disseminated from parent to child? Are social institutions like a religious organization, educational institutions, the media, or other various sources of information the expected means of providing guidelines about the appropriate behavior and expected routines the form sexual scripts. The degree to which such expectations and interactions are formal or informal remains something that needs to be understood.

In the case of the émigré, the structural elements may not exist in the United States. This loss simply means that alternatives need to be developed. The issues of both language as well as reference to values or beliefs that have been brought by the person to the United States remains something that deserves consideration. Not all Hispanics possess competence and comfortableness in speaking American English. Similarly, in many locations it is possible to obtain materials and speak most of the time in some version of Spanish and therefore minimize the exposure to language. With the growth of Latino channels on cable television and broadcast radio, the Hispanic population in the United States increasingly does not have to rely on the use of American English to communicate with others.

The problem is not simply one of translation of material from one language to another and then simply retransmitting the material. The rules for appropriate communication in Latino culture involve a different set of social norms that may not simply permit a simple translation of materials to accomplish the goals.

The problem for various ethnic and minority groups is that the traditional cultural traditions and mores no longer have the same meaning or value when transplanted into the context of the United States. Each group and each person must develop and find an identity that adapts to the changing circumstances. Many minority groups are not made up of a single ethnic or culturally homogeneous group. In fact, many of the groups have deep-seeded animosities relating to historical events in the distance or even immediate past. The problem is that the representation of these groups is extremely difficult because the assumptions about acculturation may be resisted as each group desires to develop an independent and unique identity.

The function of identity for both the individual as a person, but at the same time connected to a shared identity of the culture, could be labeled a dialectical form of tension. Even accepting the definition of cultural preferences for collectivism and individuality simply define the endpoints or preferred points of a continuum, they do not avoid the essential contradiction that a person faces. There exists the need for the individual to create a sense of identity that is unique and individual, but at the same time needs to fit within a context and conform to some shared set of values and actions to gain strength from membership in a collective.

A central issue is the extent to which a particular culture group feels as if it has acculturated to values thought to be American versus retaining a sense of identify based on the culture from the nation of ethnic origin. The focus on sexual issues makes the problem more manifest because many cultural patterns are associated with sexual behavior and the appropriateness of various behaviors.

The importance of a positive racial group orientation should not be underestimated. Persons with a positive view of their own racial group have a better self-concept, are more likely to succeed in education, use less drugs, and are less likely to violate the law. The problem with acculturation as a process is that, in some manner, an image or identity must be modified because of the need to adapt to another dominant culture. This process of adaptation can be painful as both the immigrant seeks acceptance from the larger community but also must create a sense of self-acceptance. The process of acculturation will involve uneven application of ideas from the dominant culture as the person tries to integrate existing beliefs with the new ones encountered.

The tension that exists between the cultural tradition, as a part of the ethnic identity, and the larger majority sexual culture reflects a problem of identity that requires management by individuals. The conflict is exacerbated by the problem of HIV infection because education and prevention efforts often run contrary to accepted or established cultural patterns for sexual interaction. Abraham and Sheeran (1994) indicate the need to develop a means of modeling and ultimately modifying the sexual behavior of heterosexuals (the same application would exist for heterosexuals as well). Croteau et al., (1993) point out the need to develop sources of information and education that work within the cultural setting rather than against the cultural norms and practices.

The choice of message delivery system must reflect the cultural preference and existing means of obtaining various forms of information. The current research on media consumption patterns when linked to an understanding of how groups use the media to obtain information and achieve other goals deserves continued attention and development. Targets groups must be provided messages in a setting and manner that fits within the natural ecology of the use of media as well as the nature of interpersonal relationships that currently exist. The problem with not working within the current framework is that the messages are going to be ineffective, for no other reason than they will not be accessed by the target population.

The understanding of sexual practices of the various groups in the society will increase the eventual effectiveness of educational methods. Sexual practices should be considered something that people prepare for, consistent with a view of appropriate sexual practice. Sexual behavior has elements of physiology related to psychological evaluations as well as fantasy and imagination. The satisfactory sexual experience combine elements of physiological, psychological behaviors that reflect both individual and social expectations for the event. Any effective HIV education and prevention program must fit within that context and not fundamentally change the situation in a manner that prevents the participants from meeting those goals sought from the interaction.

CHAPTER SIX

Safer Sex and the Aged

HIV infection is viewed in a variety of manners. The population creates a kind of prototype or expectation about the nature of the persons that are at risk. Although some types of persons are more at risk for infection (persons engaged in anal sex, IV drug users that share needles), the reality is that anyone who is sexually active or using IV drugs has some level of risk. Groups of persons may not believe that the risk exists because of some type of assumption about the nature of the behavior or the "kinds" of persons that are involved. However, engaging in intravenous drug use and sexual intercourse provides an element of risk for all such individuals. The question of whether any particular group will accept that the behavior constitutes a risk remains an open question. The first step in effective methods of HIV education and prevention requires that a group accept that a risk exists for them. The recognition that elder Americans were not receiving attention was noticed more than a decade ago (Catania, Stall, Coates, Pehham, & Sacks, 1989; Catania, Turner, Kegeles, Stall, Pollack, & Coates, 1989). Although the recognition of the problem existed 10 years ago when about 10% of the HIV infections occurring in persons over the age of 50 (most of that to homosexual males), the problem gained little support in terms of federal spending or public attention (Shenson & Arno, 1989). For example, an examination of three books on issues dealing with social interaction (Derlega & Barbee, 1998), behavioral interventions (Kalichman, 1998), and the politics of AIDS (Elwood, 1999) contain no explicit and specific issues dealing with older persons at risk. Despite the potential size of and estimated size of the risk group, little attention has been targeted at the need for interventions and education for this population.

Probably no group is more unaware of the need to consider precautions for sexual behavior than the elderly. For the purposes of this chapter and clarity, we define this particular population as persons over the age of 50. For women, the more salient measure may be the onset of menopause, a physiological change. The reason that women may be considered different is that the lack of fertility changes the motivation and possible consequences of sexual interaction. Although men may have similar physiological changes that are ongoing, the ability to mark this change and relate any change to a demonstrable and immediately recognizable physiological outcome currently does not exist. Male aging is usually associated more with impotence, however this outcome may be ameliorated by drugs like Viagra and is considered later in terms of the medical and health issues related to older Americans.

The assumptions that most persons make is that HIV is a disease of the young and the promiscuous (or the homosexual male, intravenous drug user, prostitute, etc.) rather than a disease that impacts on persons over the age of 50 (books like those of Fumento, 1988, as well as other AIDS denialists such as Maggiore dispute the fundamental existence of any substantial risk). The representation of the disease as something associated with youth or something targeted at only gay males creates a psychological distance between the disease and recognition of risk. The image of the person infected with HIV remains that of a person relatively young (whether a heterosexual, homosexual, or even intravenous drug user, IVDU). The image of the disease creates a stereotype or an expected person that is imaged as someone that gets the disease.

Current AIDS education and prevention programs target younger ages (this is justified because of the larger element of primary risk as measured by the numbers becoming infected). However, such a targeting strategy for educational efforts means that older persons will not have the same level of message exposure. When exposure to the current set of message occurs, the images portrayed in the message will necessarily provide an image targeted toward a younger audience with different values and orientations. The impact of educational materials is to psychologically distance the audience from acceptance of the risk. The net effect is a reduction in the effectiveness of educational materials as the audience views the content as irrelevant. The very targeting of a message at the population perceived to be most at risk by its very nature contributes to convincing the rest of the population of a reduced risk. If the population were at risk, then the expectation of a generalized message targeted for everyone would be or at least should be generated.

An example of the impact of informational campaigns that can simultaneously increase acceptance for one audience while at the same time diminish the perception of risk for another audience is Earvin "Magic" Johnson's announcement that he was HIV positive. A meta-analysis of the empirical studies finds that both adults and children hearing the message gained in knowledge about the transmission of HIV (Casey et al., 2003). However, the same meta-analysis indicates that adults increased in the level of anxiety about HIV infection whereas children diminished in anxiety about HIV infection.

The results indicate that accurate knowledge about HIV made adults realize that the behaviors made them at risk. At the same time, accurate knowledge about HIV infection for children diminished the level of anxiety about risk. The children were able to identify that the behaviors that put them at risk were not behaviors that children perform. The information that hugs, shaking hands, and being physically close to another person did not cause HIV acquisition reassured children that the risk did not exist. The lesson from this announcement is that audiences do in fact assess risk on the basis of what the audience interprets as relevant. This assessment of risk indicates that the same audience may be exposed to the same message but interpret the application of risk as fundamentally different. In this case, the perception of risk increased for one group and diminished for another group. The net result of this meta-analysis should be a recognition that messages become interpreted or responded to by multiple audiences and that each such audience will provide an interpretation consistent with a vision of risk.

There exists an assessment of the material on the basis of the relevance and the importance to the particular audience. The goal of any educational campaign must involve an assessment of how such information will be made relevant and important to the target audience. An important element of the effectiveness of any fear appeal is the degree to which the risk stated in the message is determined to be relevant to the person in terms of the risk (Witte & Allen, 2000). The meta-analysis (Witte & Allen) points out that the persuasiveness of the message is an outcome, in part, to whether the message receiver believes that the risk is something likely to happen to that individual. The degree to which that circumstances and prevention is something applicable to the person bears direct consequences for the effectiveness of the message. If older Americans see messages with information that is determined to not apply to that audience, then the message will be less effective in generating the desired behavioral outcomes.

Given the recent development of drugs that diminish erectile dysfunction in men (e.g., Viagra) and the increasing number of drugs that assist women, the assumptions of sexual inactivity among the older population are stereotypes that are increasingly inaccurate. Persons of advanced years are now becoming increasingly sexually active and the ravages of time are not necessarily reducing the issues of sexually transmitted diseases. Crary (2003) reports that older Americans are dating and that many not dating would like to find a romantic partner. Older women are dating younger men with increasing frequency, exposing them to a population with a higher element of risk. There are little data on how older women view younger men in terms of sexual risk for disease or as sexual partners in general. The perception of whether the person is at risk will play an important role in the desire to consider methods of reducing HIV infection risk (condom use, reducing number of partners, etc.).

Sexuality among the elderly represents a different kind of sexual practice with different considerations. For example, the risk of pregnancy does not play much of a factor in the consideration of the consequences of the risk of negative outcomes due to sexual behavior. This is in start contrast to the expectations of those sexually active and under 30. The number one reason for using condoms has been contraception, not to reduce the risk of sexually transmitted diseases. Given the lack of concern about pregnancy, the traditional motivation for condom use does not exist in this population. The script for sexual interaction that involves a consideration of risk of pregnancy does not exist and therefore the associated script or precautions about sex may not longer function for this group.

The levels of guilt and uncertainty about sexuality are reduced. The persons are generally experienced sexually and often feel less guilt or shame about sexual behavior. Many older persons have been married and are either divorced, separated, or have a deceased spouse. In addition, any children or other responsibilities are many times diminished and the flexibility to pursue relationships is increased.

The increase in divorce rates has meant that persons in this group are not necessarily single because of the death of a spouse or because the person never married. Crary (2003) reports that the corresponding liberalized attitude toward sexual behavior has turned women from "old maids" to "emancipated feminists." This means that the lack of men at the older ages has permitted and encouraged older women to find and accept younger men as potential partners. The publicity surrounding relationships like that of entertainment celebrities Demi Moore (over 40) with 25-year-old Ashton Kutcher provides a kind of confirmation or at least the public discussion of the acceptability of such relationships. The drawback of these relationships is that the older partner finds an increased risk of STD from the younger person in a higher risk group.

Given improved health and longer lives, psychological as well as physiological improvements have created an ability and willingness to engage in relationships. There is a growing focus on the issues of communication and senior citizens (Nussbaum & Coupland, 1995). How do senior citizens relate to each other, their families, and the support system in the social network? The increased number of persons in this category reflects an interest that will continue to grow with time and importance.

The Internet has seen a particular growth in older Americans using the venue to meet persons with similar interests (Crary, 2003). The kind of isolation has been reduced and the ability to find others increased. The benefits of reduced loneliness and improved access to others must be considered in light of the increased risks of socially transmitted diseases that accompany the behaviors.

THE CHALLENGE OF THE PARENT/CHILD

Normally, one source of information about sexuality for an adolescent should be the parent. However, what sources of sexuality discussion or implications of sexual behavior does a parent rely on when considering sexual issues for the self. The problem of HIV for older persons has been to examine the source of information on sexual issues for persons their age. There has been little systematic examination about the sources of information for older individuals and the sources and flows of information.

The impact of HIV for a parent and the desire or need to inform family members represents a fundamental challenge. Disclosure rates for persons demonstrate averages that indicate a lot of nondisclosure. A meta-analysis demonstrates that about 20% of spouses do not tell their partner after testing positive for HIV (Allen, Emmers-Sommer, Bradford, & Casey, 1999). This indicates that a significant number of spouses are not informing the partner of a positive test for HIV. Considering that partner notification normally occurs for all other STDs but not for HIV means that the partner is at particular risk for infection of this disease (see the chapter on use of condoms between married couples elsewhere in this book). The disclosure rate of the HIV positive person to other family members was reported as less than the report to spouses.

The nondisclosure becomes a factor to children because the adult parent must now reveal information not only of a medical nature, but about the personal lifestyle and choices, something done with great reluctance. The problem of dealing with the issues of confidentiality in older populations plays an increasingly salient issue (Linsk, 1994). As older persons are provided various services or live in assisted living arrangements, the need for assessment of physical and mental conditions grows. The problem is that family members (particularly children) often feel the need and right of consultation, especially when this involves an older parent with diminished mental capacity.

The nondisclosure may involve additional issues, particularly those involving sexual activity. The difficulty of handling issues of a person whose mental capacity has become diminished may require some development by the social welfare system. The fact that a person may have diminished mental capacity may or may not indicate diminished physical capabilities and may or may not change the desire for sexual gratification. The problem of education for someone with less than optimal mental capabilities places some issues in the hands of the caregiver and the difficulty of a child monitoring or structuring sexual activity. Given the importance and the issue of independence for an adult about the ability to freely choose sexual partnerships and conduct, the current legal and social support networks are ill equipped to consider how to accommodate both the desires and the risk of independent behavior.

The basis of choice remains the ability of a person to acquire and use information in making an informed choice that understands the risks and outcomes. The growing senior population that has diminished mental capacity represents a group whose potential sexual practices provide a danger to both themselves and others. The balancing necessary to preserve individual choice and yet retain responsibility becomes difficult to handle. This issue represents nothing new in dealing with social work and the elderly, only that the changing circumstances now require application to a different behavior.

EDUCATION POTENTIAL

The challenge will be to generate messages designed to target this new kind of risk group. The current messages are not designed to address the specific issues encountered by this group.

The advantage of educational efforts is that such efforts may be more effective with a curious audience. Older Americans show a great deal more curiosity and uncertainty about the management of relationships, partly because a number of the persons were not so active.

The groups may not have the same sense of guilt and social inhibition about such discussions. One reason for this is the level of sexual dysfunction increases with age as well as the desire to find solutions for this condition. The focus of a person for life improvement may involve the need to find information and develop methods of restoring or improving sexual function. As this factor plays a part in the person's life, the willingness to discuss and trade information with others will continue to increase. The factor makes the potential for the population to incorporation material as a means for action potentially helpful.

A consideration in prevention is the willingness of partners to discuss use of condoms prior to sex (Allen et al., 2002). The impact of educational materials on the older persons should be greater because the resistance to such education may not be as great. The fundamental challenge of educational materials is the design and implementation of materials that will work with these groups. The perception that the group is not at risk for the disease, that an older partner is "safe," as well as a lack of general knowledge about HIV infection will all play a role in the desire to talk about condom use.

The need for targeting this community requires a careful reconsideration of general messages designed at contraception. The messages to heterosexuals can deal with multiple issues at the same time when advocating condom use the reduction in STD risk and pregnancy can be simultaneously considered. Dealing with an audience that does not ponder contraception as a consideration will change some of the messages. As the focus of the audience and the concerns change, obviously the message will have to change as well.

Educational efforts will need to target the medical community as well. A survey (Hillman & Broderick, 2002) of 40 health care providers indicates that the medical community may not be aware of the risk of HIV for elderly women. This lack of awareness probably translates into delayed diagnosis because tests may not be conducted as early. In addition, the acceptance of stereotypes and myths about older women may not encourage medical caregivers to provide information and discuss the need for prevention with women.

Hillman (1998) expresses concern that a combination of factors in the medical care community such as: ageist stereotypes, general lack of knowledge, and negative responses by patients will create problems with issues of diagnosis as well as educational difficulties The problem is that the sense of psychological distance between the elderly, the social services agencies, medical care community, and sources of social support when compared to the perception of the disease creates a gulf. Combined with a lack of emphasis or awareness on the part of public policy makers, the implications for long-term prevention through education are not favorable. The long-term difficulties posed not only for prevention, but for treatment may continue to pose a challenge to all parties for some time.

The typical services for senior citizens come from members of the social work community. The real focus for educational efforts will probably require that this community of practitioners provide information and assessment for the population. Gutheil and Chichin (1991) pointed out that this set of professionals was untrained at the time of their review. They pointed out that the period from 1987 to 1990 the *Social Work & Abstracts* did not contain a single article addressing this issue. Although that has been addressed to some degree, the earlier cited articles (Hillman, 1998; Hillman & Broderick, 2002) that come later still indicate that attention is not being paid to this population with respect to HIV education and prevention.

This problem of knowledge may be particularly acute for older Americans that are members of minority groups. McGorry and Lasker (2001) point out that elderly Latinos have less knowledge than younger Latinos. While the elderly have a great deal of information, when compared to younger Latinos, the group demonstrates more inaccurate information. This finding for Latinos is important because generally younger Latinos as a group have less accurate information than the general population (Bradford, Allen, & Emmers-Sommer, 2000). What this means for education is that some minority groups among the elderly may have particular deficits that require attention. For Latinos the issues of language and acculturation play a very important role is the level of knowledge, risk, and actions taken to prevent the spread of HIV infection (Bradford et al., 2002). Essentially, acculturation for younger Latinos meant greater knowledge of HIV infection and greater tendency to engage in sexual behavior but at the same time, the level of condom use rose. What was occurring was that the process of acculturation for younger Latinos meant greater integration into general social structures of the U.S., carrying forward both the positive (more information, increased condom use) and negative (increased amount and more diverse sexual behavior) behaviors with respect to HIV. The evidence indicates that younger persons may acculturate and adopt more typical values reflecting the U.S. where as the older population (particularly first generation) will be less likely to be flexible. The problem for general health issues for elderly minority population simply become reflected in the issues for HIV education and prevention.

The fundamental barrier that must be initially dealt with is the perception of risk. The fact is that everyone sexually active is at risk. The age is no barrier, nor does age reduce the level of risk (some would argue that medically age increases the susceptibility and probability of infection). That perception that older populations are not sexually active, promiscuous, and have easy access to medical care (due to services like Medicare or Medicaid) represent misconceptions that diminish awareness and dim the urgency of the potential problem.

MEDICAL AND HEALTH CHALLENGES

There is a growth in the industry related to the sexuality of the older person. The development of drugs that make common dysfunctions preventing sexual behavior are now becoming a vast and accepted industry. The prognosis is that sexuality (and all the potential problems associated with increased sexual activity) will continue to increase for the older populations. The possibility of pregnancy for a woman post-menopause, although a limited application (at least initially) poses another set of potential challenges and considerations for HIV prevention and education. The issue of sexuality to the older population represents a growth industry, particularly for a society that continues to value perceptions of health and youth.

The current crop of advertisements for men feature athletes and political figures targeting and developing the expectation that discussion of such conditions and behaviors are not as taboo a topic as previously considered. The increased openness to the public acceptability of the discussion of such topics provides a window of accessibility that public health campaigns can consider taking advantage of with this particular population. The window of opportunity into public discussion of the sexuality of older Americans represents the opening of a public dialog and entry to ideas not previously considered appropriate. The opening of this avenue provides an opportunity for discussions about responsible and safe sexual practices for older Americans, something that typical stereotypes would not have considered a realistic aspect of aging.

The impact of better health and better medicine to improve sexual functioning creates now an increased need to consider the impact of such behavior on sexually transmitted diseases. The expectation is that this problem or concern will grow over time. Crisologo, Campbell, and Forte (1996) pointed out that the complexities of dealing with geratic AIDS provides a problem current research models provide little authoritative information about. The current database and advice on dealing with the changing physiological and psychological issues relating age to HIV remains undeveloped. What the review indicates is that the spread of HIV to older Americans leaves the current social work system unprepared to handle the normal functions assigned to the system (education, screening and assessment, case management, counseling, caregiver support, advocacy). The lack of preparation in the current array of social services simply reflects a combination of lack of preparation for general STD issues for older Americans as well as the unknown social implications of changes in practices and health of older Americans. The sheer number of older Americans indicates that even if the percentage of those affected remained the same, the number would continue to rise. The expectation that both the number of total older Americans will rise and the percentage of those infected with HIV or at risk for HIV infection will rise means that the current lack of preparation may be problematic.

Another aspect of the development of better treatments for HIV infection is the increase in longevity that is associated with infection. Simply living longer means that persons will be capable of spreading or infecting others for longer periods of time. The association or assumption that younger persons are susceptible, but older persons are not at risk will become something that is difficult to assess. The improvement in treatments for HIV infection, combined with improved sexual functioning provides for a difficult combination. It is important to note that many older Americans have health problems and take a variety of medications, this means that a person that is "sick" and taking medications is not unusual among older Americans. HIV infected persons will not stand out or appear necessarily different from uninfected persons, especially when compared to how younger persons would view each other as potentially at risk as a sexual partner. For example, distinguishing between a person with AIDS dementia and Alzheimer's disease may prove difficult. One condition poses no risk for a sexual partner whereas the other condition does poses a risk for the sexual partner.

Such improvements in treatment are a double-edged sword because persons may believe that HIV infection is treatable and curable and reduce the precautions (Allen et al., 2002; Catz, Meredith, & Mundy, 2001). The result is that more accurate information about treatment may undermine the fear of the disease. Because the primary motivation used to encourage safer behaviors is the fear of the disease, a reduction in the fear of the disease corresponds to reduced effectiveness of the messages. Given that the population may misinterpret stories in the popular media about potential treatments and cures, the problem of misinformation and over optimistic reactions may represent a serious problem in the future.

The longer-term assessment may be far brighter, however. If the development of sexual scripts internalizes the expectation of condom use as an internalized norm (which may be true for the adolescent, Hynie et al., 1998), can that script emerge when the person is an older adult? The problem is that current research on script formation has little longitudinal examination and support. Clearly, scripts are subject to change based on circumstances, whether the scripts for sexual practices used as a teenager would reemerge years later is unclear and uncertain. One area of research would be an examination of the link between sexual practices of a person during adolescence linked to practices in later years.

The danger of making such an assumption is that the motivation for condom use when younger was for pregnancy prevention (contraception), the same motivation will not exist for the older person and the internalized norm for condom use may not reemerge. The acute need exists for a more generalized perception of sexual interaction and rituals for senior dating and sexual expectations. Because the evidence of the motivation may change, the scripts and accompanying issues for relational satisfaction and development may change as well.

The problem is that the social conventions for this group of emerging sexually active individuals have not been developed and the outcomes are uncertain. The lack of discussion or representation in the media plays one important role. The mainstream media have always served as a source of information about the perception of social practices. The unwillingness of the media to provide real emphasis on this population simply means that less uniformity about the expectations for behavior and less visible discussion and consideration of the issues will exist.

One important difference is that the new group of persons seeking companionship and romance as primary outcomes, sexual gratification seems to play a smaller or less expected part of the relational dynamic (Crary, 2003). However, as treatments and images change for the older population, the expectations for sexuality may change as well. The question is what social implications for behavioral expectations will change as the medical and health practices are modified. The expectation or focus on romance and relationships for interaction may stem from a motivation that reflects realistic physiological capabilities. The future question is whether a changing physiological standard will then reflect differences in the motivation for relationships. A person not capable of orgasm may focus on romance and companionship, but if older Americans become more capable of sexual functioning, does that mean that physiological ability will motivate persons to seek more sexual outcomes and raise the expectations about sexual interaction? For persons considering issues of STD transmission, the increased sexuality and any corresponding increase in sexual practices represents a change that increases risk of infection. Unfortunately, the studies on understanding motivation for interaction await future development and planning.

SOCIAL SCRIPT ISSUES

The problem of defining and resurrecting appropriate social scripts for an aging population remains difficult to assess. The new context of relational development for this population generates still a large amount of uncertainty. The use of the Internet represents a new technology that permits persons to find others with similar interests and backgrounds. The use of the technology among a population growing in numbers provides a means for persons to find each other and form relationships. The problem is that the finding and pairing of persons with similar interests to form relationships is different for older persons. Whereas 50% of marriages end in divorce, creating a pool of persons that are looking for partners, 50% of marriages do not end in divorce but instead end with the death of the other person. This means that a substantial number of persons may not have engaged in a great deal of dating or relationship ritual with other persons.

One significant factor is the extent of extramarital affairs and the question of whether the persons involved in those relationships generated different scripts for sexual practices than with a spouse. Bell, Buerkel-Rothfuss, and Gore (1987) pointed to the need and expectation that persons will develop idiomatic references and language for safer sex practices. Adelman (1991, 1992a, 1992b) pointed out that the development of safer sex conversations as part of the passion and romance of sexual interaction needs to become part of the expected behavioral routine. The problem is that for older persons, particularly those having been married for a long time, the behavioral routine developed with a partner will most likely not involve the use of a condom. The concept of safety in sexual behavior was manifested in the marital relationship and the belief in fidelity.

Even for those not being faithful to a spouse or partner the distinguishing between primary, secondary, and tertiary lovers provides a framework for understanding and enacting safer sex behaviors (Carballo-Dieguez, Remien, Dolezal, & Wagner, 1997; Hoff, Coates, Barrett, Collette, & Ekstrand, 1996; San Doval, Duran, O'Donnell, & O'Donnell, 1995). What happens is that a person will identify and develop sexual behavioral scripts involving safer sexual behaviors that are specific to the particular partner. For example, a spouse would not involve a condom, a secondary partner (a long-term lover) would use a condom, and a tertiary sexual partner may either involve behavior with low risk (oral sex, manual stimulation) and/or use a condom. The classification of the nature of the relationship with regards to sexual practices means that transitions as a person gets older provides less of a challenge because the appropriate script is available for use given the particular circumstances.

Experience with communication demonstrates some rather difficult issues sometimes when dealing with technical issues. Older persons resent the sometimes patronizing tone of messages, particularly with technical instructions (Thimm, Rademacher, & Kruse, 1998). Despite that tone of the possible messages, senior citizens provide an economic force that some corporations will find an attractive target. The marketplace will provide a means for persons to find each other and provide user friendly forums and techniques. The use of the marketplace to provide a service that persons seek will provide the force to make this action come forth.

One difficulty is that popular media entertainment is not targeted and often does not involve this particular segment of society. The focus for advertising is on a younger audience that spends more money and is more susceptible to advertising. That means that the transmission of social scripts cannot come from the normal assumptions about how popular media transmit information. The development of social appropriateness rules and other information on social issues often finds root in the popular culture. However, the development of social scripts will not as easily emerge from a group that uses the media in different and diverse ways.

This begins to represent a serious problem because the receptivity of the media to this audience is a function of the commercial possibilities represented by the members of this group. The set of persons that are receiving social security or approaching retirement are not attractive to the advertisers. This means that the amount of programming targeted toward this audience is smaller and the attention to the marketing and ideas concerned are different. The inattention to this set of audience members means that many of the contemporary themes may not resonate or find a lot of support in this particular group. The force guiding or shaping the development of social scripts is therefore missing and absent from the social scene.

The problem for AIDS education and prevention is not only to assist in the development of social scripts but will require an understanding of media consumption patterns. Given the lack of evidence or targeting of this audience, the reliance on traditional mechanisms remains problematic. The function of age with various outcomes related to media consumption indicates that images in the media will play a different role. The ideal world scenario would be the development of scripts and / or behavioral routines that have older Americans creating expectations and patterns that promote and expect the use of a condom using sex. The focus on protection for self and the other person then becomes an expected part of sexual interaction.

The issues of interpersonal and communication from health professionals will play a different role for this age group. The source of information, particularly diffusion of information to this group remains relatively understudied. The need to identify the outlets of information for this group represents the same fundamental challenge that exists with any other groups to accommodate the sources of information that are used. The design of health communication systems requires knowledge not only of the particular kinds of appeals or message content but the issues of placement of the message so that the audience is exposed to the message.

This problem is one that will continue to grow as the impact of HIV, particularly on minority populations, continues to grow. The impact of both age, improved treatments that increase longevity, and the increased sexuality of older Americans provides conditions that ultimately put another population at risk for infection without the population full cognizant of the extent to which that risk exists. The problem for sexuality is that one cannot speak of a generalized population in terms of practice, experience, or perception. The very intensity and importance of sexual practices is reflected in the various cultural taboos and requirements for acceptable sexual behavior. These behavioral scripts are not simply a manifestation of the actual sexual act but incorporate a number of social competencies about the appropriateness of behavior and discussion.

The next decade will require the development and attention to many groups not traditionally associated with HIV risk. Populations like those with mental disabilities represent another difficult group to educate about safer behaviors (Cambridge, 1996; Thompson, 1994). For senior populations effected by various declines in mental conditions, the difficulty of communication (as well as educational) effectiveness may require a reconsideration of basic strategies (Baxter, Braithwaite, Golish, & Olson, 2002; Orange, Van Gennep, Miller, & Johnson, 1998). When considering the various combinations of difficulties for education as well as the increase ability for sexual interaction, the future holds a great deal of challenge for creating safer conditions for a U.S. population as it continues to age. The need is simply to find ways to adapt the message to the changing conditions of an aging population. The same challenge exists for various health educational strategies for adolescents. The expectation that the same fundamental message will work for 9-year-old children as for 17-year-old adolescents would be found to be very strange. Similarly, the expectation that the same educational campaign designed for a 25-year-old will work for a 55-year-old, even if the same health issues are the same, should not be surprising.

The challenge requires that the country address the issues of sexuality of older Americans. A topic that medicine and disease has generated a salience about what was lacking in previous generations. Given the lack of attention, the formulation of expected behavioral patterns or models for sexual behavior do not exist for this population. The focus for HIV education and prevention will require the development and application of behavioral information that currently does not exist in a form permitting ready application to this population.

Safer Sex and Living With HIV/AIDS

The term *HIV positive* is perhaps one of the more interesting contradiction in terms. For nothing could probably be less positive for an individual than a test result considered positive for the presence of HIV. The results of such a test carry a number of consequences that require consideration. However, the first step in the process is the person deciding or being required to have a test conducted for HIV. Batchelor (1987) pointed out the mere act of deciding to get and go through testing can be nerve wracking and a difficult experience.

GOING OUT AND GETTING TESTED

The first step is encouraging people to get a test for HIV. The various estimates suggest that as many as 1/3 of persons with HIV do not know that they are infected. The reason for this lack of knowledge is the lack of testing. HIV is often asymptomatic for years, and even when opportunistic infections occur, the symptoms will be those of the infection and not necessarily related to problems in the immune system.

Encouraging persons at risk to get tested is one of the first steps in HIV education and prevention (even mandatory testing has been discussed and obviously rejected; Hein, 1991). HIV tests are usually conducted because: (a) the test is an expected or required part of some social or institutional process (military induction, marriage, prenatal test, etc.) or (b) conducted by an individual worried or concerned about the possibility of risk (unprotected sex, intravenous needle use). Cotton-Oldenburg, Jordan, Martin, and Sadowski (1999) examined the factors that led to women in prison to undergo voluntary HIV testing. The functions of fear and past exposure were obviously related. The motivation for testing has been extensively explored (Goodwin & Berecochea, 1994).

But even after the testing is conducted, the person must receive the answer to the test. A large number of persons will be tested for HIV and then not return for the results. The new testing procedure is much quicker and returns results in just a short time, that means a second visit is not required. The increased speed of the test should reduce the number of persons that test positive but are not aware. Cates and Handsfield (1988) consider the issues of counseling at the time of HIV testing and the impact of such counseling. The belief is that continued counseling efforts at the initial time of testing will increase the return rate for those getting tests. A major problem is that persons do not return for test results and if positive the person remains unaware of the infection. The lack of awareness means the treatment will be delayed and that the person does not realize the possibility of infecting others exists.

DEALING WITH THE POSITIVE TEST

The person told that the test for HIV is positive has undergone a life changing experience. Without a cure, the person will go through the rest of their life with a virus that may one day permit an opportunistic infection that will kill them. Some persons refer the disclosure of a positive test as "the day they died." The emotional and psychological consequences of a positive test and the potential threat to life are associated with depression and suicidal ideation.

This chapter explores the implications for relational development and sexual practices after testing HIV positive. A person that has tested positive is now a person that can potentially "inoculate" others (to use a colloquium). Not only does the person potentially risk other persons, but the person most likely to be infected is a relational partner (lover, spouse). The current set of social relationships are usually a source of comfort and support to a person, however a diagnosis of HIV infection puts uncertainty for many people about the nature of those relationships. Given that the outlook for medical treatment is improved when social support exists, the uncertainty about that support may have serious health implications for the individual as well as the associated emotional turmoil.

The first implication is whether or not the person tells the other party that they are now infected with the virus. Such an undertaking involves risk, the other person's response generally is not going to be pleasant and the person already has had the news applied to themselves. The current law permits this decision often to be a choice rather than a legal or social requirement.

TELLING THOSE YOU LOVE

In most jurisdictions, a positive STD test requires the local health department to notify sexual partners (spouses) that they have been exposed to an STD and require testing. HIV however is generally not part of the STD list that requires partner notification. Without the government agency notifying the lover(s), the responsibility falls to the individual person to provide the information. A positive test for HIV, however, in many jurisdictions falls into a zone of privacy and the lover or spouse may not be notified. Combined with the fear that persons would not get tested if mandatory partner notification occurred limits the involvement of public health services (Fordyce, Sambula, & Stoneburner, 1989). The failure to provide for partner notification means that a failure of the person that is HIV positive to tell a lover or spouse puts the other person at risk. Greene and Serovich (1996) report that persons living with AIDS (PLWA) have a variety of reactions to the expectation of disclosure of test results. PLWAs tend to find the privacy issues more relevant and feel less likely to disclose when compared to the expectations of the general population about disclosure of HIV status. One aspect of the disclosure issue is that various groups (parents, friends, health care professionals, etc.) all believe that there are different reasons for the person to be told serostatus (Greene, Parrott, & Serovich, 1993; Kimberly, Serovich, & Greene, 1995). The net result is that the decision to disclose to a spouse or long term relational partner is not something that society enforces for the person testing positive for HIV. Given the obvious risk for the other person for infection (and spouses do not generally use condoms), the decision not to tell essentially removes the choice or the ability for diminished risk to occur.

As noted in Table 7.1, a meta-analysis of disclosure rates to various sources (Allen, Emmers-Sommer, Bradford, & Casey, 1999) demonstrates a disclosure rate to spouses/ long-term lovers of 71%. That means that 29% of the sexual partners are not told that the person with whom that they are sexually active is HIV positive. The implications of this for policy are immediate and important. The discussion of privacy and partner notification (Bayer & Toomey, 1992) reach into the issues of the nature of testing and the policies associated with testing (Bayer, Levine, & Wolf, 1991; Brown, Melchoir, Reback, & Huba, 1994). The question of whether anonymity will impact on the level of participation in testing remains an important question, given the need for persons that are positive to become aware of the seroconversion. But the fact that a large percentage of persons would not be told by their spouses of a positive HIV test creates an enormous pool of persons at risk.

TABLE 7.1

Disclosure of HIV Status to Various Targets

Target of Self Disclosure	% disclosure (sample size)
Friend	80% (1065)
Sexual Partner(s)	71% (1309)
Doctor/Dentist	71% (524)
Mother	58% (725)
Coworker	56% (245)
Sibling	47% (1518)
Father	36% (618)
Grandparents	33% (102)
Employer	37% (292)
Religious Leader	18% (99)

The level of partner disclosure might appear, at first glance, to be high or something that would not be cause for much concern. However, given the number of persons that are infected with HIV, the 71% figure will translate into tens of thousands of persons with sexual partners that know they are infected with HIV and not informing the other person. Suppose that of the 1 million persons that are HIV positive in the United States that 50% of them are either married or involved in long-term relationships. Of those 500,000 persons, we could count on at least 100,000 persons not being told by their lovers or spouses of a positive test for HIV. Obviously in the long-term the partner will know as the person becomes ill or starts to go on antiviral drugs. But the risk to the partner remains, at least in the short-term. Depending on the particular sexual practices of the couple, the risk may be increased or reduced to the seronegative partner. The implication of failure to have partner notification processes (as one would do for other sexually transmitted diseases like gonorrhea and syphilis) means that thousands of persons have sexual partners (spouses) with HIV and they do not know this to be true.

The assumption that testing is a positive social process was not always universally endorsed (Beardsell, 1994). So the person becomes faced with the problem of deciding to tell the person that they are most intimate with the results of a test. The problem with such a revelation is the likely immediate admission of engaging in some risky behavior. This is in addition to the implication that the violation of relational norms has now put the partner at risk and that they should be tested. The social stigma and fear of rejection from the one person that matters most probably makes disclosure difficult. Usually disclosure also must accompany a confession of infidelity or intravenous drug use and this makes the process even more difficult.

The reality is that the partner will eventually find out about the HIV test results. However, the failure to use condoms, to get tested, and to start drug therapies means that the impact of the disease is greater than if notification occurred immediately. There exists a very real need for counseling and educational efforts simply to assist the person to develop the courage and the strength to tell a partner of a positive test for HIV. Without this necessary step, one route of the spread of the disease will be difficult to control.

RISK BEHAVIOR CHANGE

A central issue is whether persons after testing positive for HIV will diminish risk behaviors. A great deal of effort is spent after a positive test in counseling on this issue (Otten, Zaidi, Wroten, Witte, & Peterman, 1993). The goal is to have persons after a positive test result change their sexual and needle use habits. The means by which the disease infected the individual is the same manner in which that individual could infect others. The need to change behavior becomes demonstrated by a positive test, so the consideration of what scripts for interaction and behavior require modification are demonstrated.

A current meta-analysis on this issue demonstrates a reduction in risk behaviors after a positive test result (Allen et al., 1999). The measures of risk considered were the incidence of: (a) unsafe sex, (b) number of sexual partners, and (c) unsafe injection drug use. All measures demonstrate that after infection the individuals did change behavior to reduce the risk to other persons. The good news aspect of this finding is that when notified of a positive test result of HIV, the person did respond by diminishing the amount of risk behavior. The impact of HIV infection was at least a behavioral change that would put other persons less at risk.

What the overall experience indicates is that the positive test result does have the impact of reducing the level of risk that individuals engage in. The decline in risk behaviors means that the rest of the population is less at risk. However, such behaviors were not reduced to zero, the person still did engage in risk behavior. What this finding implies is that there exists still some effort necessary for educators and the health care community to improve and reduce the level of risk by targeting persons that are known to be capable of infecting others.

Of particular note is the decreased risk for injection drug users (Deren, Beardsley, Tortu, & Goldstein, 1998). When this reduction in risk can be combined with the use of needle exchange programs, the diminished rate of infection should prove remarkable. Ksobiech (2003) demonstrates using meta-analyses of program statistics that the impact of needle exchange programs is such that using the Binomial Effect Size Display (Rosenthal, 1984) that a 50% decline in HIV rates is possible.

What the evidence indicates is that the diagnosis of an HIV infection provides the basis for some fundamental changes in the way a person conducts themselves with sexual partners and with other intravenous drug users. The importance of finding means to change the various social scripts involved in the transmission of the illness from person to person indicates that such efforts are successful. The problem is that very little literature exists on the long-term implications of educational efforts with these populations. The fundamental changes in practices are not something that only occurs temporarily, the changes mark (until a cure or vaccine is developed) a permanent change. Whether the changes observed are simply temporary or limited to particular circumstances and / or partners is not clear from the current literature.

New research needs to be conducted that considers the longitudinal aspects of changes in behavior following HIV infection. A necessary examination of the impact both short and long term for any observed changes or educational program. The problem is that such follow-ups cannot simply be measured in terms of a few months' time, the long-term studies must examine behavior of persons infected with HIV for long periods of time (literally years). The need for this effort will be ongoing, the existence of new treatments so far has not lessened the ability of a person to spread the disease. Although improvements in current treatment reduce the probability of death, the impact on the life of the person and the potential health threat remains grave.

REPRODUCTIVE DECISIONS

The decision about whether to have a child or what to do with existing children provides a challenge for any parent. Ahuluwalia, DeVellis, and Thomas (1998) point out that for women the need to consider the implications is very important. The problem is that HIV/AIDS has some important implications both long term and short term for the sexually active and fertile woman. For women who may have been planning to have children, seropositivity now represents a multifold risk. First, the virus may prove fatal to the person. Second, the virus may be transmitted to any potential child (use of drugs during pregnancy reduces this risk-but the drugs are strong and may impact the pregnancy). Finally, any potential uninfected father is put at risk during the process of natural conception. The risks are all potential risks and any of the outcomes are very uncertain and not perfectly known.

Agne, Thompson, and Cusella (2000) reported that many persons are not comfortable discussing HIV issues with health care providers. The fear of stigma or rejection by the members of the health care system means that such discussions often do not occur with persons or agencies that can best advise the individual. When this is combined with a sense of social isolation, the results for effective and planned decisions are reduced. This is particularly true for women considering issues about child bearing, the medical community may not be supportive or question the desire given the infection. This means that the medical community may be viewed by some with suspicion and mistrust and the creation of a barrier to effective advice may exist.

For a woman, the decision about reproduction is complicated because one method of HIV transmission is from mother to child (either through breastfeeding or by blood in the womb). The desire to have a child requires the mother run the risk of infecting the child. In addition, a male that is not HIV+ may be at risk in contracting HIV from the women during conception. The challenge for the person is how to manage and come to terms with the issues of conception and reproduction. Bedimo, Bessinger, and Kissinger, (1998) pointed out the choices that a woman makes during this time will vary and be related to a number of factors and decisions. The problem is that the current system of health care is not configured to permit a full and thorough examination of all the factors that would contribute to this decision.

A long-term concern emerges because the woman must decide about the issues of care during the illness. In Africa, it is sometimes true that the only time a person is likely to receive drugs is during pregnancy to reduce the risk to the unborn child. Such a position privileges pregnancy and creates an interesting standard because of the implications for the value of a mother (but only during one part of the process). In the United States, the pregnant woman may face a dim prospect with reduced access to abortion and unsupportive governmental systems that do not permit or encourage long term consideration of child rearing or resources for the care of the child.

Finally, the woman must consider what provisions to make in case HIV becomes AIDS and life threatening. A child (or children) must be provided for after the death of the woman. The stress of finding long-term care for children simply adds to both the level of guilt and stress felt by the mother. Given the uncertain legal and other statuses because of the unknown length of the infection, the process of planning represents a difficult process. The woman must take care of her own future and then consider the potential future of the children and the father. The problem is one that current social services and health care are poorly equipped to consider, let alone recommend advice or counsel.

Parents are also faced with the difficult disclosure to uninfected children (Leslie, Stein, & Rotheram-Borus, 2002; Schrimshaw & Siegel, 2002). There is only now beginning some programs to deal with parents infected with HIV (Forehand, Steele, Armistead, Morse, Simon, & Clark, 1998). The question of what to tell a child, and at what age becomes a source of stress and concern for any parent facing a terminal or long-term infection. The consideration that parents owe to tell children about the infection becomes another source of stress in the family and must be considered in the context of both general health issues and reproduction.

The move from treating HIV as an illness of an individual to a more systemic approach that deals more holistically with the family represents a move in health care of more systemic views of long-term illness in general. A similar view of Alzheimer's as a disease where much of the care will come from family members (spouses, siblings, children) involves nothing new but instead represents a view to the past, when family took more direct responsibility for the care of other family members. Given the escalating cost of institutional settings for care, the need to recognize and train families for care has become recognized and increasingly endorsed.

The current set of social services and family law is ill equipped to advise or to handle this unique set of challenges faced by the population. The current legal system does not prohibit or provide for dealing with the nature of the changing status of the HIV infected individual. A separate educational program for both women considering having children after infection needs to be considered. At the same time, women testing positive for HIV need to have appropriate information made available about the risk of pregnancy as well as medical information about the ability to protect a fetus and the problems and issues that confront long-term care for both the parent and the child.

SOCIAL SUPPORT

A serious or terminal illness creates a fundamental life changing event that the person must consider. The threat of a long illness as well as the issues of medication and seeking appropriate medical care become paramount. To counter the potential depression and negative emotional outcomes, most persons would seek and expect social support from family and friends. Schwarzer and Leppin (1989) pointed out that there is a connection between positive health outcomes and the receipt of social support. Essentially, social support functions to help individuals and reduces feelings of stress and discomfort. The result is that both the body and mind respond positively and a person physically and emotionally feels better.

However, seeking support from others is difficult for a person with HIV, as to receive social support a person must reveal the status. The lack of disclosure of the viral infection means that the availability of social support may be questionable or even absent in many cases. The person testing positive for HIV is faced with the dilemma of revealing the infection of a disease that inevitably prompts the question, "how did you catch it?" For many persons, such a question implies the admission or implies that the person was involved in something anti-social or violated some relational or social taboo. However, failure to make such a revelation means that the social system of the individual remains unaware of the infection and cannot be accessed as a means of support.

Additionally, the uncertainty of the reaction of others mitigates against disclosure. HIV is an illness that is acquired through a limited number of identifiable and specific behaviors (unsafe sex, intravenous needles). The disclosure of illness comes with the accompanying questions about the method or means of acquisition. The disclosure involves questions about the nature of the transmission and the possible relational transgressions or lifestyle implications of such information. The inevitable series of potentially embarrassing questions means that the motivation to seek social support from family, friends, and co-workers may not be available for many individuals. Schneider et al., (1991) pointed out that the level of suicidal ideation tends to be greater when a sense of social isolation exists. The result of lack of social support may be not only a lack of positive benefits from various medical treatments but an increase level of suicide attempts and depression from the diagnosis.

For homosexuals, the disclosure involves not simply the disclosure of an illness, but may reveal aspects a life lived in the closet. Gay males may not be "out" to others like family or at work. The disclosure of the infection, even if not accompanied by a discussion of the means of transmission, will prompt a number of attributions and speculations about the lifestyle and choices of a person. The risk for the gay male becomes not only the lack of support for the disease but the additional number of persons that may find the "secret lifestyle" something to condemn. When AIDS first originated some referred to it as the "gay plague" conjuring up an image of Biblical torment sent by God as a revenge against transgression. The fear that persons may view the individual in a similar vein forestalls efforts at seeking social support. The critical feature is that the person has generated an image that people have accepted that is a departure from reality. When social support is sought the

combination of redefining the image of the person as well as the consequences of infection requires a great deal of acceptance. In essence, the social
network members will often feel deceived and misled, rather than viewing
the pain of the discloser, the members of the network may feel as though
they have been in part victimized. The net result is a social network that is
less supportive than it would have been with another disease like leukemia
or prostate cancer.

For example, when Earvin "Magic" Johnson announced he was HIV positive, there was considerable speculation that he might be gay or bisexual.
However, because he as a well-respected athlete and could document a number of heterosexual acts, the speculation was very short-lived. What was not
however reduced was the level of social support that he received for the condition and health challenges that he faced during the illness. His professional
basketball career was terminated but he still continued to play, despite facing a
number of serious questions and challenges by others to the appropriateness
of his engaging in sports with others. The struggle of Magic Johnson to gain a
measure of acceptance from those in his profession as well as members of the
public (and he started from a position of high acceptance and positive celebrity) still represented something difficult to overcome.

The stigma or associated sense of homophobia can lead others to not want
to associate or be present with a person that is HIV positive. The fear of the virus and the panic that the condition may be transmitted creates a reaction at
such a visceral level that the infected person may not feel comfortable or encounter a great deal of negative reactions from others. Mason, Marks, Simoni,
Ruiz, and Richardson (1995) pointed out the idea that nondisclosure may be a
culturally sanctioned secret for Latinos. Essentially, as long as the fact is not
made public, then it can be ignored or at least the family and friends do not
have to formally accept the fact that the male is gay. But the impact of this kind
of treatment is to further make the disease invisible, education impossible or
unnecessary (no one needs or requires education if no one is infected). The result is that any desire of the person to discuss or confide or seek overt social
support is left without options because public discussion of the disease is either
forbidden or simply not recognized.

Even when additional support is gained, the stress on the individuals providing support and care requires examination. Nurses caring for AIDS patients
exhibit a great deal of stress (Klonoff & Ewers, 1990). Takigiku, Brubaker, and
Hennon (1993) documented the stress among family members as caregivers.
The problem with both groups of caregivers is that the stress of a long-term
and potentially fatal illness tends to wear down and reduce the ability of the
family member to provide support and care over time.

CONCLUSION

The means of acquisition may focus the person on accusations toward others as well as accusations from others toward the self. The process of HIV infection may fundamentally indicate a misplaced trust or create a lack of trust from others if disclosure occurs. The problems of the changes in behavior necessary after a person becomes infected simply reflect the general problems associated with the disease. The means of transmission generally reflects various issues that reflect a developed lifestyle and patterns of sexual behavior. Although changing some of the behavior is probably possible, the immediate cessation of behaviors may be unlikely. The need for education and support requires an openness that the mere diagnosis of the disease prevents. Unlike other STDs, this one is wrapped in shadows and privacy because of the assumption of shame. The image of the disease is reinforced by the very privacy laws intended to protect the individual. The result is a confusing set of contradictory images, legal policies, and assumptions that appear difficult to sort out. On the one hand, privacy rights are to be respected, but at the same time the law says one cannot discriminate on the basis of the disease (and knowledge of status is required before you can discriminate).

The problems of testing positive begin a process of ascertaining what changes become necessary in the life of a person. The reexamination of the fundamental assumptions of the life for that person is in order. The implications for education are both encouraging and difficult. The person must consider changes in behaviors and practices that may not have been previously accessible to outside agencies or persons. The necessity of change for both the health of the person and for those around the person represent an opportunity for education. The focus on education and counseling at this moment represents an opportunity for consideration and change. Given that previous evidence in the Allen et al. (1999) meta-analysis suggests that such changes do take place, the opportunity is a real one and seized by many. The challenge is finding a method of improving the effectiveness of ongoing interventions to reduce the spread of the illness. The research must consider the dynamics of ongoing changes in medicine as well as ongoing changes in the communities affected or most at risk. The opportunity to reduce infection is one that can be realized and one that should not be missed.

The life of the individual changes as the need for medical care and social support increases. Consideration must now be paid to changing elements of the life in order to accommodate the needs of treatment and the side effects of the various antiviral therapies. Given the side effects of various treatments and the sometimes strict regimen that must be followed, social support would seem essential to permit persons to cope and continue with a positive frame of mind.

The need for education and prevention is more acute for this group. This group is at risk for secondary infection as well as presents a risk of infecting other persons. The effectiveness of such efforts has been documented. Given the ability to be effective with the group that should be targeted the most, the policy implications for education and prevention become clear.

Associated with the questions of education and practices after a positive outcome is the need for education and identification of persons that do not provide names of contacts after an HIV test (Pope et al., 1992). One doctor working in an HIV clinic told the authors that, "you basically put a person in a hammerlock to get them to tell you who they have been with." One way around the rules has been the fact that HIV is an STD and often the person testing positive for HIV will also test positive for a different STD. The other STDs are usually covered under the mandatory partner notification act and the partner can be required to come in for testing. When the partner does come in for testing the doctor will recommend that an "additional" HIV test be conducted "just to make sure." This recommendation for an additional test at least provides the opportunity for the medical staff to determine if the person is currently infected with HIV. At the same time, the medical staff tells the person that the law does not permit them to reveal a positive test for HIV from the "contact" that named them. The recommendation by the staff then is to use safer sexual practices to prevent the potential risk of HIV infection, which coincidently is spread in the same manner as the disease that for which they are currently being tested. The result is a system of public health care that can achieve the ends of HIV prevention and education without violated the rules of privacy or confidentiality that are in place. At the same time the public health community is trying to convey the potential seriousness of the situation to the person.

The need for some educational approaches is particularly acute given the ability to inform current sexual partners or potential future partners does not exist in most jurisdictions. The stress on responsibility becomes important, given many jurisdictions provide for sex as a crime if the partner is not informed. However, this punitive approach must be used judiciously and with some caution, the assumption that the person is a criminal and therefore a social outcast can reaffirm the sense of isolation and feelings of social outcast. One of the worst possible outcomes would be a population of infected persons that fear testing and the implications of a HIV positive designation. The implications are persons that would avoid testing and refuse or conceal the results of that testing from all persons.

The current approach seems to be fairly punitive based on the assumption that violations of the law involve putting others unknowingly at risk. In other words, a person living with HIV having unprotected sex with another person uninfected is a crime (in some places) but only if the presence of the infection is not revealed. The assumption is that a person will be deterred from infecting another person because of the risk of criminal sanction from the lack of disclosure. The problem with the logic of that approach is that for many persons with HIV infection, the threat of going to prison loses the deterrence that laws are generally supposed to generate. If the person feels that the disease is a life sentence, then the threat of prison represents something not credible as a deterrent on the mere face of it.

The logic of the approach places a premium on voluntary disclosure and the assumption that fear of prison and appropriate education will promote such behavior. Clearly, the current research does demonstrate that after testing positive persons do diminish the level of risk behaviors, particularly when some type of intervention is ongoing (Allen et al., 1992; Sahlu et al., 1999).

The problem is that this approach obviously does not work for everyone. The dilemma that comes from this is the question of whether the introduction of a Scarlett letter should be undertaken. The Scarlett letter "A" refers to the requirement that a person convicted of adultery would wear a large scarlet "A" on their clothing to identify them as a transgressor. Clearly, this approach would not be feasible or possible, however given the real risk that someone who is HIV positive (could deliberately or unintentionally) infect someone remains a real possibility.

The problem with HIV is that unlike other STDs, the virus cannot be cured and represents both a short and long term health threat. Although HIV infection is no longer considered an immediate death sentence, the risk of serious health complications as well as expensive treatment remains. The fact that the virus can continue to be infectious to others months and even years later indicates a permanent change in the relationship of a person to others. Unlike many conditions, the assumption of an extended duration is becoming a reality as treatments improve for the conditions and methods found to strengthen the immune system.

The limited nature of the means by which the virus is spread however makes the threat manageable. But the social stigma of HIV/AIDS makes the admission of infection difficult to disclose. What happens is that the person is aware of the risk from behavior but unwilling to take a test that may generate an outcome that requires a public admission of the past behavior. Given the difficulty of admission and the opportunity for denial, the problems of generating safer outcomes will remain a difficult one. The problem is acute, because the persons HIV positive are the ones that spread the virus.

What happens is that instead of open discussions and concern for the past relationships of the persons and the need for effective treatment, the past becomes a source of shame. The development of the condition is something to hide from others. The greatest needs of the individual for social support and acceptance and the need of the society to educate and reduce the spread of the infection are contradicted by the need for privacy. The question of balance and how to establish a sense of negotiated boundaries is real (Petronio, 1991). The need of society and the individual must find a course that balances the desires and needs of both bodies. HIV infection tests those boundaries because the sexual practices of the individual impact public health. That does not mean that public health requirements must dominate the expectation and assumption of privacy that a person has about sexual practices. However, HIV does represent at the current time a unique challenge in that the traditional policies and assumptions do not seem to create mechanisms for handling the epidemic. Society must reexamine the assumptions about the privacy of all sexual behavior and the consistency of social policy on this issue. Failure to do so means that more than 20% of spouses (partners) of HIV infected individuals will falsely assume they have nothing to fear. Conversely, persons with HIV will assume that disclosure means that they have everything to fear. Until the policy and society find a way to create a technique to handle the fear the current educational policies, while providing some positive effect, will remain largely ineffective and resolving this threat to the public health.

Conclusion

BRINGING IT ALL TOGETHER

Several conclusions can be drawn from the previous chapters. First and foremost, HIV affects everyone in some fashion or another, whether it is personally, relationally, socially, economically, or politically. Many, perhaps, perceive HIV and AIDS as being a problem "overseas" (e.g., Africa, Asia, India). We must not be so ethnocentric and narrow as to perceive HIV and AIDS as a problem solely affecting non-western, non-industrial, underdeveloped countries. Indeed, even as the authors were writing this text, the number of HIV and AIDS cases increased worldwide and also in the United States. For example, the AIDS figure reported in chapter 1 was 774,467 and the number of cases reported through 2001 was 816,149 (CDC, 2003b). Thus, even as this book evolved, so did the number of HIV and AIDS cases and they continue to do so. As indicated next, many groups often dismissed in terms of the dialogue about HIV and AIDS are quite affected. According to the CDC's (2002b) Surveillance Report:

> Of all HIV infections in 2001, 39% progressed to AIDS within 12 months after diagnosis of HIV infection. AIDS was diagnosed within 12 months after the diagnosis of HIV infection for a larger proportion of older persons (35 and older), Hispanics, Asians/Pacific Islanders, American Indians/Alaskan Natives, IDUs, and persons exposed through heterosexual contact. (p. 6)

As indicated earlier, within the United States, HIV and AIDS are typically referenced in the same breath as men having sex with men. Not addressed as readily are older adults, heterosexuals, or individuals from various cultural backgrounds. As acknowledged by the CDC (2003b), "The AIDS epidemic is far from over" (¶ 2). Until that day when a cure or effective vaccine is found, propositions are offered as a synthesized reflection of what has been addressed in the preceding chapters.

HIV Is Not Relationship Specific.   As indicated in the various chapters, HIV and AIDS are not specific to heterosexual dating relationships, marital relationships, homosexual male relationships, bisexual relationships, or even lesbian relationships. Although incidence among the latter group is less prominent, risk does exist when certain sexual practices are exercised. Similarly, just as HIV and AIDS are not specific to any particular relational group, no group is immune, either. According to the CDC's (2002b) Surveillance Report, between 1998 and 2001, AIDS declined among men having sex with men, IV drug users, and men having sex with men who were also IV drug users. By 2002, AIDS among men having sex with men increased slightly. Among heterosexuals, however, AIDS increased each year between 1998 and 2002. What the statistics reflect is a changing nature of the disease, various populations by failing to diminish risk are becoming increasingly infected in the United States. The impact of the change is to increase the scope of the disease to have a larger percentage of the population at increased risk. The failure to take action to diminish the risk of infection will mean that inevitably larger numbers of more diverse parts of the population will demonstrate increased infection.

It is important for scholars and laypersons alike to approach HIV and AIDS from a more unified perspective. As mentioned in chapter 2, individuals' mobilizing to protect and reinforce group identity can be harmful in such attitudes and behavior perpetuates that myth that HIV and AIDS are "gay issues". Indeed, as presented in this text, that is not the case. It is important to recognize that HIV and AIDS are universal; thus, we coexist in the same group from that perspective. It is also important, however, to recognize that there may be certain communicative and behavioral practices that are more specific to one group over another. The importance of recognizing this from a theoretical, script perspective is that educational programs, campaigns, and interventions can take population-specific attitudes and behaviors into account when creating messages that will resonate most strongly with that population. The problem is a classic dilemma of having a problem that is universal, because the disease transmission occurs in every group but at the same time generating effective prevention and education programs that work with particular populations. The challenge for the application of social science requires the simultaneous creation of universal or generalizable understandings that improve the formulation of practice but at the same time find a means of application that permit the adaptability or specificity of the message as provided to various elements of the community. The recognition that a message must be adapted for particular cultures or groups is nothing new, but the current regimens are less than effective in routinely recognizing and incorporating this as a fundamental feature. The usual practice is that more like a fire fighter, the fire fighter goes to where the fires are and puts them out. Such a model if reactive, not proactive to the problem of prevention. Money and efforts that went to prevention and education for gay men now are shifting to minority women and one finds an increase in risk in gay men. The problem is that with limited resources, the targeting of populations perceived most in need is prudent, but as with any form of education, each generation must go through the process and the entire effort recreated to maintain effectiveness. The current strategy of focus on the most at risk populations works when the issues of disease control are short-term, however, for longer-term issues like HIV infection, a reconsideration of fundamental approach deserves attention.

HIV Is Not Gender Specific.   As mentioned in chapter 4, HIV and AIDS were originally approached and spun politically as a gay male's disease. As demonstrated in this text and as disseminated publicly, however, HIV and AIDS affect both men and women. As indicated, whereas incidence of HIV might be tapering off for adult gay males (compared to its peak), HIV/AIDS incidence increased for men having sex with men each year between 1999-2002 (CDC, 2002b). Similarly, HIV is on the rise for gay adolescent males and is on the rise for heterosexual women. In fact, since 1985, the proportion of all AIDS cases reported among adolescent and adult women in the United States more than tripled. In 1999, within the United States, HIV and AIDS was the fifth leading cause of death among women aged 25 to 44 and the third leading cause of death among African American women (CDC, 2003b). According to the 2002 Surveillance Report (CDC, 2002b), 79% of the new cases of HIV/AIDS in 2002 were due to men having sex with men (44%) or individuals exposed through heterosexual contact (35%). Overall, between 1998-2002, AIDS diagnoses increased by 7% for women and decreased by 5% for men (CDC, 2002b).

From a script perspective, much work is needed to make safer sex talk and practice more a part of our social and relational consciousness. As indicated in chapter 4, safer sex discussion and practice has become part of the relational tapestry in adult male gay relationships. This script has held less of an impact in adolescent gay male relationships for a variety of reasons, including more of a reliance on antiretroviral therapies and the fact that these adolescents were not old enough to experience the influx of HIV and AIDS that impacted the gay male community so severely in the 1980s. Thus, although all of these men might be gay males, their worlds differ in some respects as they relate to the experience of HIV and AIDS. Older gay males often talk about the sadness, loss, and fear of the disease in the mid-1980s as the epidemic swept through the population. Current young gay men do not share that experience and lack the fundamental emotional orientation to the onset of the disease as the older generation. Younger gay men grew up during a time when there always was HIV, and fewer people die from ARC now, the immediate sense of threat is simply not a part of the underlying vocabulary or affect.

As indicated in chapters 2 and 3, HIV and AIDS are also a heterosexual problem, whether the relationship in question is a dating or marital one. As indicated earlier, of particular concern are men's and women's adherence to traditional sexual scripts. Such scripts are sexually confining, oppressing, and divisive. Specifically, heterosexual men are socialized to be sexually conquering; sometimes, such socialization can result in diminutive attitudes toward women and sexual relationships or manifests itself in the form of coercive behavior. Women, on the other hand, are socialized to be relational harmonizers and gatekeepers. Women are taught to keep the peace, ensuring that others are happy, even if the other's happiness might result in compromising her health and well being. The combination has women put in control of sexual behaviors but at the same time put in a position of perceived lower power and unable to make or enforce decisions.

It is important for *both* men and women to feel comfortable saying "no". From a more socially stereotypical standpoint, it is important that men feel comfortable not pursuing sex, particularly if conditions exist that put them at risk. For women, it is important that they do not "give in" due to badgering for sex or concern that the partner's feelings are going to be hurt or egos offended if sex is denied or if sex is agreed to only if safety measures are practiced. Of course, converse scenarios could exist as well (i.e., where the woman is the pursuer and the man is the recipient of the overtures). Bottom line, protecting yourself should take center stage over protecting relationships, social perceptions, and so on. Related, one must question a relationship and a relational partner if he or she is not concerned with your well being. In summary, as safer sex practices become more a part of relational talk, such discussions will become more interwoven into the social and relational tapestry. The adult gay male community provides a good example of how to incorporate such a script and how to feel comfortable with it. Gay men did it because it became a matter of survival for the community. In reality, everyone should engage in these conversations. The impact of such a conversation is an increase in the probability of condom use which translates into diminished risk of HIV infection. The conversation apparently does matter in relation to the behavior, however creating the basis for that conversation as part of the cultural practices still seems elusive.

HIV Is Not Culturally Specific. As indicated in chapter 5, HIV is not specific to non-western, more economically compromised, oppressed countries or cultures. Whereas it is true that HIV and AIDS are more prominent in Af-

rica than the United States, and incidence is growing in India and Asia (particular concerns about China for the future), it is important that HIV and AIDS are
recognized as a global issue. Although economic and political implications exist for the United States by affected countries, such implications—in addition
to personal and relational implications—exist for individuals in the United
States. These implications are currently more pronounced for Blacks and Hispanics in the United States. Of all AIDS cases reported in 2001, 68% of the affected individuals were Black and Hispanic adults and adolescents (CDC,
2003a). The CDC (2002a) reports that HIV-related death is most pronounced
among racial and ethnic minorities. Since 1991, HIV has been the leading
cause of death in African-American men aged 25 to 44 (CDC, 2002a) and, as
mentioned above, the third leading cause of death in African-American
women (CDC, 2002a, 2003a). Generally, an argument can be made in the
United States the minority groups (particularly those with lower average in-
comes) are becoming increasingly affected by the spread of the virus.

According to the CDC, although African American and Hispanic women
account for less than ¼ of all United States women, they constitute 78% of
AIDS cases in the United States. According to the CDC's (2002) Surveillance
Report, HIV and AIDS among whites, Hispanics, and Asians/Pacific Island-
ers increased and remained stable for blacks. However, over half (54%) of
the new diagnoses of HIV/AIDS in 2002 were among Blacks. In 2000, Hispanic and Black women represented 80% of AIDS cases in women (CDC,
2003b). What this indicates is that persons of color, often the least noticed or
powerful in the society, are generating the largest number of new cases of
HIV. The increased attention for prevention and education is warranted.
The increased infection rates should indicate the needs to change the perception of the disease and the need to reach out to populations often more difficult to find and educate.

Many issues need to be taken into consideration when addressing HIV and
AIDS among various ethnic groups. First, educational and intervention efforts
need to be aware of cultural issues such that messages resonate more readily
with various ethnic groups. These messages can be integrated into sexual
scripts. Second, it is important to consider groups more afflicted by HIV and
AIDS as co-cultures versus subcultures. This line of thinking will assist in elim-
inating the notion that HIV and AIDS are group-specific or population specific
issues. The fundamental problem in the United States is that these cultures do
not exist as geographically separated groups, the cultures of the various ethnic
and racial groups often exist together in the same city or community. Even in
large cites, the separation or segregation to a small part of the community only
indicates a concentration in a particular neighborhood. The health care sys-

tem and mass communication systems are still often shared and more in common at a mass level than specific (although some specialized media do exist and patterns of consumption may vary).

HIV Is Not Age Specific.   HIV is a growing problem among adolescents and among the aged. According to the CDC (2002a), 31,293 cases of AIDS existed for young individuals aged 13 to 24. According to Rosenberg, Biggar, & Goedert, 1994, cited in CDC 2002a), at least half of the new HIV infections in the United States are among individuals under 25, most of whom acquired HIV through sexual infection. AIDS incidence increased among 13 to 14 and 15 to 24 year olds. When considering the areas of the United States that engage in confidential HIV reporting for adolescents and adults in 2000, the statistics for young individuals are concerning, particularly for young women. Specifically, between the ages of 13 and 19, a greater percentage of HIV cases were among females (i.e., 61%) than males (i.e., 39%; CDC, 2002a).

To address these issues among children and young adults, educational programs should be integrated in health education classes at schools such that discussion of safer sex practices become more readily integrated into the sexual script. The CDC (2002a) suggests starting programs on health related behaviors as young as kindergarten and that school health programs are aligned with parental and community values. Comprehensive programs that espouse delaying sexual activity and then engaged in safer sexual practices once activity has begun are the most effective types of programs (CDC, 2002a). The CDC also recognizes that many youth in the most need of such educational services might not be privy to them for homeless, runaway, dropouts, offenders, and so on. Community based services need to be made available for such individuals. Finally, the CDC recommends that drug related risk be addressed in prevention programs. Statistics indicate that 1 in 50 high school students have engaged in IV drug use. This has lead to HIV infection due to IV drug use alone in young individuals aged 13 to 24 in 2000 and 50% of the sexually transmitted cases of HIV (in states tracking HIV among adolescents and adults; CDC, 2000).

The problem with adolescent education efforts is that the scripts necessary for safer sexual practices run counter to existing social scripts that recommend chastity and virginity. The challenge for educational efforts is whether both scripts can simultaneously exist in the same educational system or community. The problem for many adolescents is that the conflict between the expectation of virginity (from school, parents, religion, government) and the pressures for sexual exploration and expression (popular culture, peers, physical gratification) create a series of inconsistent messages. The failure to provide a means of integration has meant that adolescents are left with conflicting scripts or representations about the appropriateness of various actions. The result is often failure to plan sexual encounters or the "blame" of drugs (alcohol, ecstasy, marijuana, cocaine, etc.) for failure to enact safer behaviors. What transpires is a hodge-podge of inconsistent behavior set within the context of shame, guilt, rebellion, and thrill-seeking. Adolescents represent one of the most difficult groups for prevention and education efforts because of the nature of all the contradictions (including inexperience) that exist in the formulation of such scripts.

As indicated earlier, HIV and AIDS are also an issue among older Americans. The number of AIDS cases among those age 50 and older is increasing (Catania, Turner, Kegeles, Stall, Pollack, & Coates, 1989). According to the CDC (2002b), AIDS incidence increased among individuals in the 45 to 54, 55 to 64, and 65 years and older age groups. In fact, 41% of the new AIDS diagnoses in 2002 were among individuals aged 35 to 44. Survival rates decreased as age at diagnosis increased among persons aged at least 35 at diagnosis (CDC, 2002b). Indeed, among more aged adults, it is important to instill the need for individuals to include safer sex talk into their script. The perception of the disease as something that impacts on the young and promiscuous (particularly the gay man or the intravenous drug user) permits the older population to perceive a condition that is not relevant to their practices. Part of the perception may be reflected in the idea that the older person is more experienced and better able to make judgments and therefore unlikely to make the mistakes of youth.

The initiation of new sexual relationships is likely on the rise for a number of relational partnerships involving older individuals. For example, entering the "dating scene" after the dissolution of a marriage is not uncommon due to the high incidence of divorce in the United States (i.e., approximately 50%) or due to the death of a spouse. In addition, the propensity to seek or pursue sexual relationships may be intensified due to the availability of sexual enhancement drugs, such as Viagra. For women, use of sexual enhancement medications is an issue as well as the fact that many postmenopausal women might not feel the need to use condoms because pregnancy is no longer an option. As mentioned in chapters 2 and 3, many adults perceive condoms primarily as barrier method birth control measures as opposed to also recognizing their utility as reducing HIV and STDs. Another issue to consider is that it is not uncommon for men or women to date a partner who is younger than him or her and, as reported in chapter 6, younger partners are among higher risk groups. Regardless of conditions that brought them there, heterosexual adults must be cognizant of the fact that sexual discussions that might not have been necessary "back in the day" are now very much a reality. The ultimate truism remains, "anyone that is sexually active is at risk."

Patel (Patel & Morley, 2003) examined the sexual practices of 2000 women in the continental United States who were contacted via a random digit dialing survey. The study was conducted in 1996, before the influx of Viagra. The ages of women in Patel's study ranged from 18 to 94. Patel found that frequency of sexual activity as well as condom use decreased with age. In the study, Patel found that 12% of sexually active married women over the age of 60 reported condom use. Patel noted that women might be using condoms to reduce STD/HIV risk or to prolong partner erection. Morley (cited in Dotinga, 2003) indicated that safer sex needs to be an issue with senior men as well, noting that prostitution arrests rise around the country when the government distributes social security checks. Stall and Catania (1994) observed that although a reasonable percentage of AIDS cases in the United States are among Americans aged 50 and older, little attention has focused on sexual behaviors for middle-aged or older Americans. The result is an invisible population that is at risk for infection but receives relatively little attention. The inattention, in part, is simply the belief that sexual activity is something for the young and does not concern older Americans.

Overall, both young and old need to integrate safer sex discussion and sexual history discussion into their script. For younger individuals, assuming that safer sex talk and practice is unnecessary due to the antiretroviral therapies available constitutes an error in knowledge. Specifically, the therapies are meant to assist in managing living with HIV and AIDS, but they are not a cure. Although the drugs may permit many to function, the side effects and other restrictions mean that a person may not have the quality of life that existed prior to infection. The cost of the treatment must be paid by someone, and the drug therapies are not cheap and require strict adherence. Additionally, secondary infection is a possibility such that the newly acquired strain of HIV is not treated by the current antiretroviral therapy taken by the individual. Also, the infected person must take precautions to minimize the risk to others, something that is not always implemented.

For more aged individuals, it is important to understand that although HIV and AIDS might not have been a reality decades ago during their dating days, they must realize—just as other STDS such as syphilis and gonorrhea were an issue at the time—that a new STD has been added to the mix. Working safer sex discussions and enforcing condom use might be a greater challenge for aged women, as many might believe that such discussions are inappropriate or not lady-like. Educational interventions and programs, perhaps offered at senior centers, retirement homes, or assisted living centers would be of use and assist in integrating such discussions into the culture such that they are not perceived as uncomfortable or taboo. Additionally, medical practitioners could integrate discussions of this nature with their patients.

HIV and AIDS Are Part of Our Personal, Relational, Social, Economic, and Political Landscape.   As noted earlier, "The AIDS epidemic is far from over" (¶ 2). It is important that individuals rid of stigma associated with discussing safer sex, practicing it, and rid of the stigma associated with individuals living with HIV and AIDS. Stigmas are associated with ignorance and intolerance. As noted earlier in this text, ramifications and implications of HIV and AIDS are far-reaching and they affect us on various fronts and in various manners. For such reasons, a motivation exists to increase awareness, practice safer behaviors (e.g., condom use, be screened for HIV and other STDS, not engage in intravenous drug use, not mix drugs/alcohol with sexual situations, etc.), and to be aware when others are not engaging in such behaviors or who lack the awareness. The challenge is the need to rededicate or practice constant vigilance and necessary practices on a constant basis across a lifespan.

As noted, many individuals avoid HIV and AIDS-related issues because they perceive little risk or feel invulnerable. The myths associated with such beliefs have been offered earlier in this text. Additionally, however, individuals avoid many issues out of fear. This mentality is not absent in health-related matters, such as HIV and AIDS. Many fear the unknown and believe that not knowing is somehow a protection. For example, of the individuals who do get tested for HIV, many do not bother to find out what the results are out of fear. As indicated in chapter 7, salient issues exist and that are in need of address in the event of a positive outcome. The impact of interventions designed to promote responsible and safer behavior as well as attend to the need to start medical care early represents something very necessary beneficial.

As addressed in chapter 7, disclosure of a positive test is a personal choice— not a legal or social requirement. For individuals to feel comfortable with such a disclosure, many individuals' social and personal attitudes are in need of adjusting. If such disclosures and acceptance of such disclosures become more embedded in our social script and a more accepted part of our culture, then fear and stigmas associated with such disclosures should deplete to some extent. It is likely impossible to erase ignorance; however, ignorance is often fueled by fear and lack of education on a subject. Interventions designed to reduced the stigma of AIDS have generated mixed results (Brown et al., 2003).

Considering that some infected individuals might not divulge seropositivity status—and considering that many individuals do not know that they are seropositive—it is important for individuals to realize that they do have almost complete control over avoiding acquiring HIV. Clearly, individuals have choices as to whether or not they want to inject intravenous drugs. Individuals have the choice as to whether or not they want to engage in unprotected sexual behaviors with individuals hailing from high-risk populations. We have a choice about whether or not we choose to insist that a condom be used during a sexual encounter. Of salience is that many individuals fear HIV and AIDS because they feel powerless against them. Truth be told, however, we have much power in how we educate ourselves, how we use the information we obtain, the discussions we choose to have regarding sexual histories and safer sexual practices, and the type of sexual practices we choose to engage in and with whom. Additionally, we have a choice to get tested and make choices in terms of dealing with a positive result in terms of the therapies we seek, our maintenance of such therapies, and the engagement in safer sexual practices while living with HIV or AIDS such that we reduce risk for ourselves and others. Putting the power back to the people enables us to cope with a phenomenon that has been coined as a "war" in the media or as "out of control." In reality, we have choices at our disposal whether we are seronegative or seropositive. Recognizing the power and exercising it enables us to control, rather than be controlled.

References

Abelson, R. (1981). Psychological status of the script concept. *American Psychologist, 36,* 715–729.

Abraham, C., & Sheeran, P. (1994). Modeling and modifying young heterosexuals' HIV-preventive behaviour: A review of theories and educational implications. *Patient Education and Counseling, 73,* 173–186.

Adam, B. D., Sears, A., & Schellenberg, E. G. (2000). Accounting for unsafe sex with men who have sex with men. *Journal of Sex Research, 37,* 24–36.

Adelman, M. (1991). Play and incongruity: Framing safe-sex talk. *Health Communication, 3,* 139–155.

Adelman, M. (1992a). Sustaining passion: Eroticism and safe-sex talk. *Archives of Sexual Behavior, 21*(5), 481–494.

Adelman, M. (1992b). Healthy passions: Safer sex as play. T. Edgar, M. A. Fitzpatrick, & V. Freimuth (Eds.), *AIDS: A communication perspective* (pp. 69–89). Hillsdale, NJ: Lawrence Erlbaum Associates.

Agne, R., Thompson, T., & Cusella, L. (2000). Stigma in the line of face: Self-disclosure of patients' HIV status to health care providers. *Journal of Applied Communication Research, 28,* 235–261.

Ahuluwalia, I., DeVellis, R., & Thomas, J. (1998). Reproductive decisions of women at risk for acquiring HIV infection. *AIDS Education and Prevention, 10,* 90–97.

Ajzen, I. (1991). The theory of planned behavior. *Organizational Behavior and Human Decision Processes, 50,* 179–211.

Allen, M., & Burrell, N. (1996). Comparing the impact of homosexual and heterosexual parents on children: Meta-analysis of existing research. *Journal of Homosexuality, 32*(2), 19–36.

Allen, M., & Burrell, N. (2002). Sexual orientation of the parent: The impact on the child. In M. Allen, R. Preiss, B. Gayle, & N. Burrell (Eds.), *Interpersonal communication research: Advances through meta-analysis* (pp. 111–124). Mahwah, NJ: Lawrence Erlbaum Associates.

Allen, M., Carson, E., Chopski, K., Considine, J., Donlin, M., Gaworska, K., Huebner, B., Kopaczewski, S., Sandretti, D., & Woods, V. (2002, April). *Changing circumstances: The impact of marketing HIV treatment on AIDS education and prevention.* Paper presented at the Central States Communication Association Convention, Milwaukee, WI.

Allen, M., D'Alessio, D., & Emmers-Sommer, T. M. (1999). Reactions to criminal sexual offenders to pornography: A meta-analytic summary. In M. Roloff (Ed.), *Communication Yearbook 22* (pp. 139–169). Thousand Oaks, CA: Sage.

Allen, M., Emmers, T. M., Gebhardt, L. J., & Giery, M. (1995). Exposure to pornography and acceptance of rape myths: A research summary using meta-analysis. *Journal of Communication, 45*(1), 5–26.

Allen, M., Emmers-Sommer, T. M., Bradford, L., & Casey, M. (1999, November). *Behavior after learning positive HIV results: A meta-analysis.* Paper presented at the National Communication Association Convention, Chicago, IL.

Allen, M., Emmers-Sommer, T. M., & Crowell, T. L. (2002). Couples negotiating safer sex behaviors. In M. Allen, R. W. Preiss, B. M. Gayle, & N. Burrell (Eds.), *Interpersonal communication research: Advances through meta-analysis* (pp. 263–279). Mahwah, NJ: Lawrence Erlbaum Associates.

Allen, M., Howard, L., & Grimes, D. (1997). Racial group orientation and self-concept: Examining the relationship using meta-analysis. *Howard Journal of Communications, 8,* 371–386.

Allen, S., Tice, J., Van de Perre, P., Serufilira, A., Hudes, E., Nsengumuremyi, F., Bogaerts, J., Lindan, C., & Hulley, S. (1992). Effect of serotesting with counseling on condom use and seroconversion. *British Medical Journal, 304,* 1605–1609.

Altman, I., & Taylor, D. A. (1973). *Social penetration: The development of interpersonal relationships.* New York: Holt, Rinehart & Winston.

Attridge, M. (1994). Barriers to dissolution. In D. J. Canary & L. Stafford (Eds.), *Communication and relational maintenance* (pp. 141–164). San Diego, CA; Academic Press.

Baldwin, J., Trotter, R., Martinez, D., Stevens, S., John, D., & Brems, C. (1999). HIV/AIDS risks among Native American drug users: Key findings from focus group interviews and implications for intervention strategies. *AIDS Education and Prevention, 11,* 279–292.

Bandura, A. (1977). Self-efficacy: Toward a unifying theory of behavioral change. *Psychological Review, 84,* 191–215.

Batchelor, W. (1987). Real fears, false hopes: The human cost of AIDS antibody testings. *AIDS and Public Policy, 2,* 25–30.

Baxter, L., Braithwaite, D., Golish, T., & Olson, L. (2002). Contradictions of interaction for wives of elderly husbands with adult dementia. *Journal of Applied Communication Research, 30,* 1–26.

Baxter, L. A. (1988). Dyadic personal relationships: Measurement options. In C. H. Tardy (Ed.), *A handbook for the study of human communication methods and instruments for observing, measuring, and assessing communication processes* (pp. 193–228). Norwood, NJ: Ablex.

Baxter, L. A., & Wilmot, W. W. (1985). Taboo topics in close relationships. *Journal of Social and Personal Relationships, 2,* 253–269.

Bayer, R., Levine, C., & Wolf, S. (1991). HIV antibody screening: An ethical framework for evaluating proposed programs. In N. McKenzie (Ed.), *The AIDS reader: social, political, ethical issues* (pp. 327–346). New York: Meridian.

Bayer, R., & Toomey, K. (1992). HIV prevention and the two faces of partner notification. *American Journal of Public Health, 82,* 1158–1164.

Beardsell, S. (1994). Should wider HIV testing be encouraged on the grounds of HIV prevention? *AIDS Care, 6,* 5–19.

Bedimo, A., Bessinger, R., & Kissinger, P. (1998). Reproductive choices among HIV-positive women. *Social Science and Medicine, 46,* 171–179.

Bell, R., Buerkel-Rothfuss, N., & Gore, K. (1987). "Did you bring the yarmulke for the cabbage patch kid?" The idiomatic communication of young lovers. *Human Communication Research, 14,* 47–67.

Berscheid, E., Snyder, M., & Omoto, A. (1989). The relationship closeness inventory: Assessing the closeness of interpersonal relationships. *Journal of Personality and Social Psychology, 57,* 792–807.

Bostwick, T. D., & De Lucia, J. L. (1992). Effects of gender and specific dating behaviors on perceptions of sex willingness and date rape. *Journal of Social and Clinical Psychology, 11*, 14–25.

Bowers v. Hardwick, 106 S. Ct. 2841 (1986).

Bradford, L., Allen, M., Casey, M., & Emmers-Sommer, T. M. (2002). A meta-analysis examining the relationship between Latino acculturation levels and HIV / AIDS risk behaviors, condom use, and HIV / AIDS knowledge. *Journal of Intercultural Communication Research, 31*, 167–180.

Bradford, L., Allen, M., & Emmers-Sommer, T. M. (2000, November). *Latino HIV / AIDS knowledge and behaviors: A meta-analysis of existing research.* Paper presented at the National Communication Association Convention, Seattle, WA.

Brafford, L. J., & Beck, K. H. (1991). Development and validation of condom self-efficacy scale for college students. *College Health, 39*, 219–225.

Breakwell, G. M., Fife-Schaw, C., & Clayden, K. (1991). Risk-taking, control over partner choice and intended use of condoms by virgins. *Journal of Community and Applied Social Psychology, 1*, 173–187.

Brown, D., & Bryant, J. (1989). Uses of pornography. In D. Zillmann & J. Bryant (Eds.), *Pornography: Research advances and policy considerations* (pp. 3–24). Hillsdale, NJ: Lawrence Erlbaum Associates.

Brown, I. S. (1984). Development of a scale to measure attitude towards the condom as a method of birth control. *Journal of Sex Research, 20*, 255–263.

Brown, L., Macintyre, K., & Trujillo, L. (2003). Interventions to reduce HIV / AIDS stigma: What have we learned? *AIDS Education and Prevention, 15*, 49–69.

Brown, V., Melchoir, L., Reback, C., & Huba, G. (1994). Mandatory partner notification of HIV test results: Psychological and social issues for women. *AIDS & Public Policy Journal, 9*(2), 86–92.

Bruce, K., Shrum, J., Trefethen, C., & Slovik, L. (1990). Students' attitudes about AIDS, homosexuality, and condoms. *AIDS Education and Prevention, 2*, 220–234.

Burgoon, J. K., & Hale, J. L. (1987). Validation and measurement of the fundamental themes of relational communication. *Communication Monographs, 54*, 19–41.

Burt, M. (1980). Cultural myths and supports for rape. *Journal of Personality and Social Psychology, 38*, 217–230.

Byers, E. A. (1996). How well does the traditional sexual script explain sexual coercion? Review of a program of research. In E. S. Byers & F. O'Sullivan (Eds.), *Sexual coercion in dating relationships* (pp. 7–26). New York: Hawthorne.

Cambridge, P. (1996). Assessing and meeting needs in HIV and learning disability. *British Journal of Learning Disabilities, 24*(2), 52–57.

Carrballo-Dieguez, A., Remien, R., Dolezal, C., & Wagner, G. (1997). Unsafe sex in the primary relationship of Puerto Rican Men who have sex with men. *AIDS and Behavior, 1*, 9–17.

Carillo, E., & Urganga-McKane, S. (1994). HIV / AIDS. In C. Molino & M. Agurre-Molino (Eds.), *Latino health in the U.S.: A growing challenge* (pp. 313–337). Washington, DC: American Public Health Association.

Carroll, J., & Carroll, L. (1995). Alcohol use and risky sex among college students. *Psychological Reports, 76*, 723–726.

Casey, M. K., Allen, M., Emmers-Sommer, T. M., Sahlstein, E., Degooyer, D., Winters, M., Wagner, A. E., & Dun, T. (2003). When a celebrity contracts a disease: The example of Earvin "Magic" Johnson's announcement that he was HIV positive. *Journal of Health Communication, 8*, 249–265.

Catania, J. A., Coates, T. J., Stall, R., & Turner, H. (1992). Prevalence of AIDS-related risk factors and condom use in the United States. *Science, 258*, 1101–1106.

Catania, J. A., Stall, R., Coates, T. J., Pelham, A., & Sacks, C. (1989). Issues in primary AIDS prevention for late middle-aged and elderly Americans. *Generations, 13*, 50–54.

Catania, J. A., Turner, H., Kegeles, S. M., Stall, R., Pollack, L., & Coates, T. (1989). Older Americans and AIDS: Transmission risks and primary prevention needs. *Gerontologist, 29*, 373–381.

Cates, W., & Handsfield, H. (1988). HIV counseling and testing: Does it work? *American Journal of Public Health, 78*, 1533–1534.

Catz, S., Meredith, K., & Mundy, L. (2001). Women's HIV transmission risk perceptions and behaviors in the era of potent antiretroviral therapies. *AIDS Education and Prevention, 13*, 239–251.

Centers for Disease Control (2002a). Young people at risk: HIV/AIDS among America's youth. Available online at: http://www.cdc.gov/hiv/pubs/facts/youth.htm

Centers Centers for Disease Control (2002b). HIV/AIDS Surveillance Report, Vol. 14.

Centers for Disease Control (2002, June 6). Slide Set: HIV/AIDS General Epidemiology: Updated Through 2000. Retrieved on June 11, 2002 from the Internet at http://www.cdc.gov/hiv/graphics/surveill.htm

Centers for Disease Control (2003a). HIV/AIDS Among US Women: Minority and Young Women at Continuing Risk. Available online at: http://www.cdc.gov/hiv/pubs/facts/women.htm

Centers for Disease Control (2003b). AIDS in Blacks and Hispanics. Available online at: http://www.cdc.gov/hiv/graphics/images/1238/1238-3.pdf

Check, J. V., & Malamuth, N. M. (1983). Sex role stereotyping and reactions to depictions of stranger vs. acquaintance rape. *Journal of Personality and Social Psychology, 45*, 344–356.

Christiansen, M., & Lowhagen, G. (2000). Sexually transmitted diseases and sexual behavior in men attending an outpatients' clinic for gay men in Gothenburg, Sweden. *Acta Dermato-Venereologica, 80*, 136–139.

Christopher, F. S., & Frandsen, M. M. (1990). Strategies of influence in sex and dating. *Journal of Social and Personal Relationships, 7*, 89–105.

CNN Interactive (February 8, 1998). Study: Many people with AIDS virus don't tell sex partner. Available online at: http://www.cnn.com/HEALTH/9802/08/sexualethics.ap/

Cochran, S. D., & Mays, V. M. (1990). Sex, lies, and HIV. *The New England Journal of Medicine, 332*, 774–775.

Collins, R. (1998). Social identity and HIV infection: The experiences of gay men living with HIV. In V. Derlega & A. Barbee, (Eds.). *HIV & Social Interaction* (pp. 30–55). Thousand Oaks, CA: Sage.

Copeland, A. (1993). Suicide among AIDS patients. *Medical Science and Law, 33*, 21–28.

Cotton-Oldenburg, N., Jordan, B., Martin, S., & Sadowski, L. (1999). Voluntary HIV testing in prison: Do women inmates at high risk for HIV accept HIV testing. *AIDS Education and Prevention, 11*, 28–37.

Couch, L. L., & Jones, W. H. (1997). Measuring levels of trust. *Journal of Research in Personality, 31*, 319–336.

Crary, D. (2003, September 29). Survey examines attitudes of older singles: Dating and age: Midlife singles' attitudes change. *Milwaukee Journal Sentinel*, p. 5A.

Crisologo, S., Campbell, M., & Forte, J. (1996). Social work, AIDS, and the elderly: Current knowledge and practice. *Journal of Gerontological Social Work, 26*, 49–60.

Critelli, J. W., & Suire, D. M. (1998). Obstacles to condom use: The combination of other forms of birth control and short-term monogamy. *Journal of American College Health, 46*(5), 215–219.

Croteau, J., Nero, C., & Prosser, D. (1993). Social and cultural sensitivity in group-specific HIV and AIDS programming. *Journal of Counseling and Development, 71*, 290–296.

Crowell, T. L., & Emmers-Sommer, T. M. (2000). Examining condom use, self-efficacy, and coping in sexual situations. *Communication Research Reports, 17*(2), 191–202.

Crowell, T. L., & Emmers-Sommer, T. M. (2001). "If I knew then what I know now": Seropositive individuals' perceptions of partner trust, safety, and risk prior to HIV infection. *Communication Studies, 52*(4), 302–323.

Cummings, G. L., Battle, R. S., Barker, J. C., & Krasnovsky, F. M. (1999). Are African American women worried about getting AIDS? A qualitative analysis. *AIDS Education and Prevention, 11*, 331–342.

DeLamater, J. (1987). Gender differences in sexual scenarios. In K. Kelley (Ed.), *Females, males and sexuality* (pp. 127–139). Albany: State University of New York.

Deren, S., Beardsley, M., Tortu, S., & Goldstein, M. (1998). HIV serostatus and changes in risk behaviors among drug injectors and crack users. *AIDS and Behavior, 2*, 171–176.

Derlega, V., & Barbee, A. (Eds.). (1998). *HIV & Social Interaction.* Thousand Oaks, CA: Sage.

Dotinga, R. (2003, March 14). Sex wanes with age, women say. Available online at: http://www.healthfinder.gov/news/newsstory.asp?docID=512213

Doval, A., Duran, R., O'Donnell, L., & O'Donnell, C. (1995). Barriers to condom use in primary and nonprimary relationships among Hispanice STD clinic patients. *Hispanic Journal of the Behavioral Sciences, 17*, 385–387.

Duncan, D. (1990). Pornography as a source of sex information for university students. *Psychological Reports, 66*, 442.

Duncan, D., & Donnelly, J. (1991). Pornography as a source of sex information for students at a private Northeastern university. *Psychological Reports, 68*, 782.

Duncan, D., & Nicholson, T. (1991). Pornography as a source of sex information for students at a Southeastern university. *Psychological Reports, 68*, 802.

Ebron, A. (1999, April 1). What your kids want to know about sex, drugs, and violence. *Family Circle, 112*, 44–46.

Edgar, T., Freimuth, V., Hammond, S., McDonald, D., & Fink, E. (1992). Strategic sexual communication: Condom use resistance and response. *Health Communication, 4*, 83–104.

Ehde, D. M., Holm, J. C., & Robbins, G. M. (1995). The impact of Magic Johnson's HIV serostatus disclosure on unmarried college students' HIV knowledge, attitudes, risk perception and sexual behavior. *Journal of American College Health, 44*(2), 55–58.

Elford, J., Bolding, G., Maguire, M., & Sherr, L. (1999). Sexual risk behavior among gay men in a relationship. *AIDS, 13*, 1407–1411.

Ellen, J. M., Vittinghoff, E., Bolan, G., Boyer, C. B., & Padian, N. S. (1998). Individuals' perceptions about their sex partners' risk behaviors. *Journal of Sex Research, 35*, 328–332.

Elwood, W. (Ed.). (1999). *Power in the blood: A handbook on AIDS, politics, and communication.* Mahwah, NJ: Lawrence Erlbaum Associates.

Elwood, W., & Williams, M. (1999). The politics of silence: Communicative rules and HIV prevention issues in the male bathhouses. In E. Elwood (Ed.), *Power in the blood: A handbook of AIDS, politics and communication* (pp. 121–132). Mahwah, NJ: Lawrence Erlbaum Associates.

Emling, S. (2000, January 17). Cheating hearts make good business. Retrieved on January 17, 2000 from the Internet at http://www.usatoday.com/life/ldso26.htm

Emmers, T. M., & Dindia, K. (1995). The effect of relational stage and intimacy on touch: An extension of Guerrero and Andersen. *Personal Relationships, 2*(3), 225–236.

Emmers, T. M., & Canary, D. J. (1996). The effect of uncertainty reducing strategies on young couples' relational repair and intimacy. *Communication Quarterly, 44*(2), 166–182.

Emmers-Sommer, T. M. (2002). Sexual coercion and resistance. In M. Allen, R. W. Preiss, B. M. Gayle, & N. Burrell (Eds.), *Interpersonal communication: Advances in meta-analysis* (pp. 315–343). NJ: Lawrence Erlbaum Associates.

Emmers-Sommer, T. M., & Allen, M. (1999). Variables related to sexual coercion: A path model. *Journal of Social and Personal Relationships, 16*(5), 659–678.

Emmers-Sommer, T. M., & Allen, M. (2001). HIV and AIDS: Toward increased awareness and understanding of prevention and education using meta-analysis. *Communication Studies, 52*(2), 127–140.

Emmers-Sommer, T. M., & Crowell, T. L. (1999, May). *"I'm certain there's nothing to be uncertain about": The effect of reasons for condom-use suggestion on certainty, trust, and intimacy in marital relationships.* Paper presented at the International Communication Association Conference, San Francisco, CA.

Festinger, L. (1954). A theory of social comparison processes. *Human Relations, 7,* 117–140.

Fishbein, M., & Ajzen, I. (1975). *Beliefs, attitude, intention, and behavior: An introduction to theory and research.* Reading, MA: Addison-Wesley.

Fitzpatrick, M. A. (1987). Marriage and verbal intimacy. In V. J. Derlega & J. Berg (Eds.), *Self-disclosure: Theory and research* (pp. 191–217). New York: Plenum Press.

Fordyce, E., Sambula, S., & Stoneburner, R. (1989). Mandatory reporting of human immunodeficiency virus testing would deter Blacks and Hispanics from being tested. *Journal of The American Medical Association, 262,* 349.

Forehand, R., Steele, R., Armistead, L., Morse, E., Simon, P., & Clark, L. (1998). The family health project: Psychosocial adjustment of children whose mothers are HIV infected. *Journal of Consulting and Clinical Psychology, 66,* 515–520.

Freimuth, V. S., Hammond, S. L., Edgar, T., McDonald, D. A., & Fink, E. L. (1992). Factors explaining intent, discussion and use of condoms in first time sexual encounters. *Health Education Research, 7,* 203–215.

Frith, H., & Kitzinger, C. (2001). Reformulating sexual script theory: Developing a discursive psychology of sexual negotiation. *Theory and Psychology, 11,* 209–232.

Fumento, M. (1988). *The myth of heterosexual AIDS: How a tragedy has been distorted by the media and partisan politics.* New York: Basic Books.

Gagnon, J., & Simon, W. (1973). *Sexual conduct: The social sources of human sexuality.* Chicago, IL: Aldine.

Gagnon, M., & Godin, G. (2000). The impact of new antiretroviral treatments on college students' intention to use a condom with a new sexual partner. *AIDS Education and Prevention, 12,* 239–251.

Gibson, F. X., Gerrard, M., Lando, H. A., & McGovern, P. G. (1991). Social comparison and smoking cessation: The role of the "typical smoker." *Journal of Experimental Social Psychology, 27,* 239–258.

Glass, R. (1988). AIDS and suicide. *Journal of the American Medical Association, 259,* 1369–1370.

Glass, S. P., & Wright, T. L. (1997). Reconstructing marriages after the trauma of infidelity. In W. K. Halford & H. J. Markman (Eds.), Clinical handbook of marriage and couples interventions (pp. 471–507). New York: Jossey-Bass.

Godin, G., & Kok, G. (1996). The theory of planned behavior: A review of its applications to health-related behaviors. *American Journal of Health Promotion, 11,* 87–98.

Goodwin, E., & Berecochea, J. (1994). Predictors of HIV testing among runaway and homeless adolescents. *Journal of Adolescent Health, 15,* 566–572.

Greene, J. (1984). A cognitive approach to human communication: An action assembly theory. *Communication Monographs, 51,* 289–306.

Greene, K., & Serovich, J. (1996). Appropriateness of disclosure of HIV testing information: The perspective of PLWAs. *Journal of Applied Communication Research, 24,* 50–65.

Greene, K., Parrott, R., & Serovich, J. (1993). Privacy, HIV testing, and AIDS: College students' versus parents' perspectives. *Health Communication, 5,* 59–74.

Gutheil, I., & Chichin, E. (1991). AIDS, older people, and social work. *Health and Social Work, 16,* 237–246.

Hale, J., Householder, B., & Greene, K. (2003). The theory of reasoned action. In J. Dillard & M. Pfau (Eds.), *The persuasion handbook: Developments in theory and practice* (pp. 259–288). Thousand Oaks, CA: Sage.

Hausenblas, H., Carron, A., & Mack, D. (1997). Application of the theories of reasoned action and planned behavior to exercise behavior: A meta-analysis. *Journal of Sports & Exercise Psychology, 19,* 36–51.

Hatfield, E., & Rapson, R. L. (1987). Gender differences in love an intimacy: The fantasy vs. the reality. *Journal of Social Work and Human Sexuality, 5,* 12–26.

Hein, K. (1991). Mandatory HIV testing of youth: A lose-lose proposition. *Journal of the American Medical Association, 266,* 2430–2431.

Helgeson, V. S., Shaver, P., & Dryer, M. (1987). Prototypes of intimacy and distance in same-sex relationships. *Journal of Social and Personal Relationships, 4,* 195–233.

Hendrick, S., & Hendrick, C. (1992). (Eds.). *Liking, loving, and relating.* Pacific Grove, CA: Brooks/Cole Publishing.

Herrett-Skjellum, J., & Allen, M. (1996). Television programming and sexual stereotypes: A meta-analysis. In B. Burleson (Ed.), *Communication Yearbook 19* (pp. 157–186). Thousand Oaks, CA: Sage.

Hillis, S. D., Marchblanks, P. A., Tylor, L. R., & Peterson, H. B. (1999). Poststerilization regret: Findings from the United States collaborative review of sterilization. *Obstetrics and Gynecology, 93,* 889.

Hillman, J. (1998). Some issues in the assessment of HIV among older adult patients. *Psychotherapy: Theory, research, practice, training, 35*(4), 483–489.

Hillman, J., & Broderick, K. (2002). HIV among elderly women: Ignored and overlooked by health care providers and public policy makers. In L. Collins & M. Dunlap (Eds.), *Charting a new course for feminist psychology* (pp. 193–215). Westport, CT: Praeger Publishers/Greenwood Publishing.

Hingson, R., Strunin, L., Berlin, B., & Heeren, T. (1990). Beliefs about AIDS, use of alcohol and drugs, and unprotected sex among Massachusetts adolescents. *American Journal of Public Health, 80,* 295–299.

Hoff, C., Coates, T., Barrett, D., Collette, L., & Ekstrand, M. (1996). Differences between gay men in primary relationships and single men: Implications for prevention. *AIDS Education and Prevention, 8,* 546–559.

Hynie, M., Lydon, J. E., Coté, S., & Wiener, S. (1998). Relational sexual scripts and women's condom use: The importance of internalized norms. *Journal of Sex Research, 35*(4), 370–380.

Icard, L. (1986). Black gay men and conflicting social identities: Sexual orientation versus racial identity. *Journal of Social Work and Human Sexuality, 4,* 83–93.

Ishii-Kuntz, M., Whitbeck, I. B., & Simons, R. I. (1990). AIDS and perceived change in sexual practice: An analysis of a college student sample from California and Iowa. *Journal of Applied Social Psychology, 20,* 1301–1321.

Johnson, S. (1987). Factors related to the intolerance of AIDS victims. *Journal of the Scientific Study of Religion, 26,* 105–110.

Kalichman, S. (1998). *Preventing AIDS: A sourcebook for behavioral interventions.* Mahwah, NJ: Lawrence Erlbaum Associates.

Katz, B. P., Fortenberry, J. D., Zimet, G. D., Blythe, M. J., & Orr, D. P. (2000). Partner-specific relationship characteristics and condom use among young people with sexually transmitted diseases. *Journal of Sex Research, 37,* 69–75.

Kellermann, K. (1991). The conversation MOP: II. Progression through scenes of discourse. *Human Communication Research, 17,* 385–414.

Kim, M., & Hunter, J. (1993a). Attitude-behavior relations: A meta-analysis of attitudinal relevance and topic. *Journal of Communication, 43,* 101–143.

Kim, M., & Hunter, J. (1993b). Relationships among attitudes, behavioral intentions, and behavior. *Communication Research, 20,* 331–364.

Kimberly, J., Serovich, J., & Greene, K. (1995). Disclosure of HIV-positive status: Five women's stories. *Family Relations, 44,* 316–322.

King, D. L. (2004). *On the down low.* New York: Random House.

Kippax, S., Crawford, J., Davis, M., Rodden, P., & Dowsett, G. (1993). Sustaining safe sex: A longitudinal study of a sample of homosexual men. *AIDS, 7,* 257–263.

Kippax, S., Noble, J., Prestage, G., Crawford, J., Campbell, D., Baxter, D., & Cooper, D. (1997). Sexual negotiation n the AIDS era: Negotiated safety revisited. *AIDS, 11,* 191–197.

Klein, W. M., & Weinstein, N. D. (1998). Social comparison and unrealistic optimism about personal risk. In B. P. Buunk & F. X. Gibson (Eds.), *Health, coping, and well-being: Perspectives from social comparison theory* (pp. 26–61). Hillsdale, NJ: Lawrence Erlbaum Associates.

Klonoff, E., & Ewers, D. (1990). Care of AIDS patients as a source of stress to nursing staff. *AIDS Education and Prevention, 2,* 338–348.

Knapp, M. L., & Taylor, E. H. (1994). Commitment and its communication in romantic relationships. In A. L. Weber & J. H. Harvey (Eds.), *Perspectives on close relationships* (pp. 153–175). Boston, MA: Allyn & Bacon.

Koss, M. P. (1988). Hidden rape: Incidence, prevalence, and descriptive characteristics of sexual aggression and victimization in a national sample of college students. In A. W. Burgess (Ed.), *Sexual assault* Vol. 2 (pp. 3–25). New York: Garland.

Koss, M. P., Gidycz, C. A., & Wisniewski, N. (1987). The scope of rape: Incidence and prevalence of sexual aggression and victimization in a national sample of higher education students. *Journal of Consulting and Clinical Psychology, 55,* 162–170.

Ksobiech, K. (2003). A meta-analysis of needle sharing, lending, and borrowing behaviors of needle exchange program attenders. *AIDS Education and Prevention, 15,* 237–268.

Larzelere, R. E., & Huston, T. L. (1980). The dyadic trust scale: Towards understanding interpersonal trust in close relationships. *Journal of Marriage and The Family, 42,* 595–604.

Lear, D. (1995). Sexual communication in the age of AIDS: The construction of risk and trust among young adults. *Social Science Medicine, 41,* 1331–1323.

Leslie, M., Stein, J., & Rotheram-Borus, M. (2002). The impact of coping strategies, personal relationships, and emotional distress on health-related outcomes of parents living with HIV or AIDS. *Journal of Personal and Social Relationships, 19,* 67–86.

Linsk, N. (1994). HIV and the elderly. *Families in Society, 75,* 362–372.

Lucchetti, A. (1998). *Deception in disclosing one's sexual history.* Paper presented at the National Communication Association Convention, New York City.

MacLachlan, M. (1997). *Culture and health.* New York: John Wiley & Sons.

Mancoske, R., Wadsworth, C., Dugas, D., & Haney, J. (1995). Suicide risk among people living with AIDS. *Social Work, 40,* 783–787.

Mandler, J. (1984). *Stories, scripts, and scenes: Aspects of schema theory.* Hillsdale, NJ: Lawrence Erlbaum Associates.

Marin, G., Sabogal, F., Marin, B., Otero-Sabogal, R., & Perez-Stable, E. (1987). Development of a short acculturation scale for Hispanics. *Hispanic Journal of the Behavioral Sciences, 9,* 18–205.

Marston, P. J., Hecht, M. L., Manke, M. L., McDaniel, S. & Reeder, H. (1998). The subjective experience of intimacy, passion, and commitment in heterosexual loving relationships. *Personal Relationships, 5,* 15–30.

Mason, H., Marks, G., Simoni, J., Ruiz, M., & Richardson, J. (1995). Culturally sanctioned secrets? Latino men's nondisclosure of HIV infection to family, friends, and lovers. *Health Psychology, 14,* 6–12.

Materre, M. (2004, February 26). On the down low. Available online at: http://wgntv.trb.com/wgntv-news-022604downlow,0,4747128.story?coll=wgntv-home-1

Maticka-Tyndale, E. (1991). Sexual scripts and AIDS prevention: Variations in adherence to safer-sex guidelines by heterosexual adolescents. *Journal of Sex Research, 28*(1), 45–66.

Mays, V., & Cochran, S. (1988). Issues in the perception of AIDS risk and risk reduction activities by Black and Hispanic/Latina women. *American Psychologist, 43*, 949–957.

Mazur, M. (2001). *An examination of parental knowledge about adolescent media consumption and parental mediation.* Unpublished doctoral dissertation. University of Oklahoma.

McCoy, C., & Inciardi, J. (1995). *Sex, drugs, and the continuing spread of AIDS.* Los Angeles, CA: Roxbury Publishing Company.

McGorry, S., & Lasker, J. (2001). Elderly Latinos in the U.S.: What do they know and think about HIV/AIDS? *Journal of Nonprofit & Public Sector Marketing, 9*(3), 89–103.

Metts, S. (1994). Relational transgressions. In W. R. Cupach & B. H. Spitzberg (Eds.), *The darkside of interpersonal communication* (pp. 217–239). Hillsdale, NJ: Lawrence Erlbaum Associates.

Metts, S., & Fitzpatrick, M. A. (1992). Thinking about safer sex: The risky business of "knowing your partner" advice. In T. Edgar, M. A. Fitzpatrick, & V. S. Freimuth (Eds.), *AIDS: A communication perspective* (pp. 1–19). Hillsdale, NJ: Lawrence Erlbaum Associates.

Metts, S., & Spitzberg, B. H. (1996). Sexual communication in interpersonal contexts: A script-based approach. In B. R. Burleson (Ed.), *Communication Yearbook 19* (pp. 49–91). Thousand Oaks, CA: Sage.

Miller, R. S., & Lefcourt, H. M. (1982). The assessment of social intimacy. *Journal of Personality Assessment, 46*, 514–518.

Misovich, S. J., Fisher, J. D., & Fisher, W. A. (1997). Close relationships and elevated HIV risk behavior: Evidence and possible underlying psychological processes. *Review of General Psychology, 1*, 72–107.

Mongeau, P. A., & Carey, C. M. (1996). Who's wooing whom II?: An investigation of date-initiation and expectancy violation. *Western Journal of Communication, 60*, 195–213.

Muehlenhard, C. L. (1988). Misinterpreting dating behaviors and the risk of date rape. *Journal of Social and Clinical Psychology, 6*, 20–37.

Muehlenharad, C. L., & Schrag, J. L. (1991). Nonviolent sexual coercion. In A. Parrot & L. Bechhofer (Eds.), *Acquaintance rape: The hidden crime* (pp. 115–128). New York: Wiley.

Muehlenhard, C. L., Friedman, D. E., & Thomas, C. M. (1985). Is date rape justifiable? The effects of dating activity, who initiated, who paid, and men's attitudes toward women. *Psychology of Women Quarterly, 9*, 297–310.

Nussbaum, J., & Coupland, J. (Eds.). (1995). *Handbook of communication and aging.* New York: Harper.

Orange, J., Van Gennep, K., Miller, L., & Johnson, A. (1998). Resolution of communication breakdown in dementia of the Alzheimer's type: A longitudinal study. *Journal of Applied Communication Research, 26*, 120–138.

Otten, M., Zaidi, A., Wroten, J., Witte, J., & Peterman, T. (1993). Changes in sexually transmitted disease rates after HIV testing and posttest counseling, Miami, 1988 to 1989. *American Journal of Public Health, 83*, 529–533.

Patel, D., & Morley, J. E. (2003). Sexual behavior of older women: Results of a random-digit-dialing survey of 2000 women in the United States. *Sexually Transmitted Diseases, 30*, 216–220.

Perper, T., & Weis, D. L. (1987). Proceptive and rejective strategies of U.S. and Canadian College Women. *Journal of Sex Research, 23*(4), 455–480.

Perry, M., Solomon, L., Winett, R., Kelly, J., Roffman, R., Desiderato, L., Kalichman, S., Sikkema, K., Norman, A., Short, B., & Stevenson, L. (1994). High risk sexual behavior and alcohol consumption among bar-going gay men. *AIDS, 8*, 1321–1324.

Petronio, S. (1991). Communication boundary management: A theoretical model of managing disclosure of private information between marital couples. *Communication Theory, 1,* 311–335.

Pilkington, C., J., Kern, W., & Indest, D. (1994). Is safer sex necessary with a "safe" partner?: Condom use romantic feelings. *The Journal of Sex Research, 31,* 203–210.

Pittman, F. (1989). *Private lies: Infidelity and the betrayal of intimacy.* New York: W. W. Norton.

Pope, S., Koopman, J., Ostrow, D., Joseph, J., Fletcher, D., Prokopowicz, G., & Natale, J. (1992). The link between sexually transmitted disease clinics and HIV counseling and testing centers: Who is not getting referred? *AIDS Education and Prevention, 4,* 219–226.

Raghubir, P., & Menon, G. (1998). AIDS and me, never the twain shall meet: The effects of information accessibility on judgments of risk and advertising effectiveness. *Journal of Consumer Research, 25,* 52–63.

Randall, D., & Wolff, J. (1994). The time interval in the intention-behavior relationship: Meta-analysis. *British Journal of Social Psychology, 33,* 405–418.

Reiss, I. L., & Leik, R. K. (1989). Evaluating strategies to avoid AIDS: Number of partners versus use of condoms. *Journal of Sex Research, 4,* 411–433.

Rempel, J. K., Holmes, J. G., & Zanna, M. P. (1985). Trust in close relationships. *Journal of Personality and Social Psychology, 49,* 95–112.

Roche, J. P., & Ramsey, T. W. (1993). Premarital sexuality: A five-year follow-up study of attitudes and behavior by dating stage. *Adolescence, 28,* 67–80.

Rogers, E. (1995). *Diffusion of innovations* (4th ed.). New York: Free Press.

Rogers, E., & Shefner-Rogers, C. (1999). Diffusion of innovations and HIV / AIDS prevention research. In W. Elwood (Ed.), *Power in the blood: A handbook on AIDS, politics, and communication* (pp. 405–414). Mahwah, NJ: Lawrence Erlbaum Publishers.

Roscoe, B., Cavanaugh, L. E., & Kennedy, D. R. (1988). Dating infidelity: Behaviors, reasons, and consequences. *Adolescence, 23,* 35–43.

Rose, S. (1998). Searching for the meaning of AIDS: Issues effecting seropositive Black gay men. In V. Derlega & A. Barbee, (Eds.). *HIV & Social Interaction* (pp. 56–82). Thousand Oaks, CA: Sage.

Rosenthal, R. (1984). *Meta-analytic procedures for social research.* Beverly Hills, CA: Sage.

Rye, B. J. (1998). The impact and AIDS prevention video on AIDS-related perceptions. *The Canadian Journal of Human Sexuality, 7,* 19–30.

Sahlu, T., Kassa, E., Agonafer, T., Tsegaye, A., de Wit, T., Gebremarian, H., Doorly, R., Spijkerman, I., Yeneneh, H., Coutinho, R., & Fontanet, A. (1999). Sexual behaviors, perception of risk of HIV infection, and factors associated with attending HIV post-test counseling in Ethiopia. *AIDS, 13,* 1263–1272.

Sanders, G. S. (1982). Social comparison and perceptions of health and illness. In G. S. Sanders & J. Suls (Eds.), *Social psychology and health of illness* (pp. 129–157). Hillsdale, NJ: Lawrence Erlbaum Associates.

San Doval, A., Duran, R., O'Donnell, L., & O'Donnell, C. (1995). Barriers to condom use in primary and nonprimary relationships among Hispanic STD clinic patients. *Hispanic Journal of Behavioral Sciences, 17,* 385–397.

Schank, R. (1982). *Dynamic memory: A theory of reminding and learning in computers and people.* Cambridge, England: Cambridge University Press.

Schneider, S., Taylor, S., Hammen, C., Kemeny, M., & Dudley, J. (1991). Factors influencing suicide intent in gay and bisexual suicide ideators: Differing models for men with and without human immunodeficiency virus. *Journal of Personality and Social Psychology, 61,* 776–788.

Schönbach, P. (1990). *Account episodes: The management or escalation of conflict.* Cambridge, England: Cambridge University Press.

Schrimshaw, E., & Siegel, K. (2002). HIV-infected mothers' disclosure to their uninfected children: Rates, reasons, and reactions. *Journal of Personal and Social Relationships, 19,* 45–66.

Schwarzer, R., & Leppin, A. (1989). Social support and health: A meta-analysis. *Psychology and Health, 3,* 1–15.

Sheeran, P., & Orbell, S. (1998). Do intentions predict condom use? Meta-analysis and examination of sex moderator variables. *British Journal of Social Psychology, 37,* 231–250.

Sheeran, P., & Taylor, S. (1999). Predicting intentions to use condoms: A meta-analysis and comparison of the theories of Reasoned Action and Planned Behavior. *Journal of Applied Social Psychology, 29,* 1624–1675.

Shenson, D., & Arno, P. (1989). AIDS, elders, and federal spending, *Generations, 13,* 28–31.

Sheppard, B., Hartwick, J., & Warshaw, P. (1988). The theory of reasoned action: A meta-analysis of past research with recommendations for modifications and future research. *Journal of Consumer Research, 5,* 325–343.

Shervington, D. (1993). The acceptability of the female condom among the low-income African-American women. *Journal of the National Medical Association, 85,* 341–347.

Shilts, R. (1987). *And the band played on: Politics, people, and the AIDS epidemic.* New York: Penguin Books.

Shimanoff, S. (1980). *Communication rules: Theory and research.* Beverly Hills, CA: Sage.

Simon, W., & Gagnon, J. H. (1984). Sexual scripts. *Society, 22,* 52–60.

Simon, W., & Gagnon, J. H. (1986). Sexual scripts: Permanence and change. *Archives of Sexual Behavior, 15,* 97–120.

Simon, W., & Gagnon, J. H. (1987). A sexual scripts approach. In J. H. Greer & W. T. O'Donohue (Eds.), *Theories of human sexuality* (pp. 363–383). New York: Plenum.

Sonnex, C., Hart, G. J., Williams, P., & Adler, M. W. (1989). Condom use by heterosexuals attending a department of GUM: Attitudes and behavior in the light of HIV infection. *Genitourinary Medicine, 65,* 248–251.

Spanier, G. B., & Margolis, R. L. (1983). Marital separation and extramarital sexual behavior. *Journal of Social Issues, 33,* 101–125.

Spinelli, A., Talamanca, I. F., Lauria, L. (2000). Patterns of contraception use in 5 European countries. European study group on infertility and subfecundity. *American Journal of Public Health, 90,* 1403.

Stall, R., & Catania, J. (1994). AIDS risk behaviors among late middle-aged and elderly Americans. The national AIDS behavioral surveys. *Archives of internal medicine, 154,* 57–63.

Steel, J. L. (1991). Interpersonal correlated of trust and self-disclosure. *Psychological Reports, 68,* 1319–1320.

Stebleton, M., & Rothenberger, J. (1993). Truth or consequences: Dishonesty in dating and HIV/AIDS—related issues in a college population. *Journal of American College Health, 42,* 51–54.

Sternberg, S. (2002, July 8). Most HIV-positive males in the USA don't know it. Retrieved on July 8, 2002 from the Internet at: http://usatoday.com/news/healthscience/health/aids/2002-07-08-us-aids.htm

Strasburger, V. C., & Donnerstein, E. (1999). Children, adolescents, and the media: Issues and solutions. *Pediatrics, 103*(1), 129–139.

Tajfel, H., & Turner, J. C. (1979). An integrative theory of intergroup conflict. In W. C. Austin & S. Worchel (Eds.), *The social psychology of intergroup relations* (pp. 33–53). Monterey, CA; Brooks/Cole.

Takigiku, S., Brubaker, T., & Hennon, C. (1993). A contextual model of stress among parent caregivers of gay sons with AIDS. *AIDS Education and Prevention, 5*, 25–42.

The Alan Guttmacher Institute (AGI) (2002). *In their own right: Addressing the sexual and reproductive health needs of American men*, New York: AGI.

Thimm, C., Rademacher, U., & Kruse, L. (1998). Age stereotypes and patronizing messages: Features of age-adapted speech in technical instructions to the elderly. *Journal of Applied Communication Research, 26*, 66–82.

Thompson, A. P. (1983). Extramarital sex: A review of the research literature. *Journal of Sex Research, 19*, 1–22.

Thompson, D. (1994). The sexual experiences of men with learning disabilities having sex with men: Issues for HIV prevention. *Sexuality and Disability, 12*, 221–242.

Tigges, B. B., Wills, T. A., & Link, B. G. (1998). Social comparison, the threat of AIDS, and adolescent condom use. *Journal of Applied Social Psychology, 28*, 861–887.

Timmins, P., Gallois, C., McCamish, M., & Terry, D. (1996, May). *Sources of information about HIV/AIDS and perceived risk of infection among heterosexual young adults: 1989-1994.* Paper presented at the International Communication Association Conference, Chicago, IL.

Treffke, H., Tiggemann, M. & Ross, M. W. (1992). The relationship between attitude assertiveness and condom use. *Psychology and Health, 6*, 45–52.

Wegscheider-Cruse, S. (1988). *Coupleship.* Deerfield Beach, FL: Health Communications.

Whittier, D., & Simon, W. (2001). The fuzzy matrix of "my type" in intrapsychic sexual scripting. *Sexualities, 4*, 139–165.

Wiederman, M. W. (1997). Extramarital sex: Prevalence and correlates in a national survey. *Journal of Sex Research, 34*, 167–174.

Willing, C. (1994). Marital discourse and condom use. In P. Aggeton, P., Davie, & G. Hart, *AIDS: Foundations for the future* (pp. 110–121). London: Taylor & Francis.

Wills, T. A. (1981). Downward comparison principles in social psychology. *Psychological Bulletin, 90*, 245–271.

Witte, K., & Allen, M. (2000). A meta-analysis of fear appeals: Implications for effective health campaigns. *Health Education and Behavior, 27*, 591–615.

Wood, J. V., Taylor, S. E., & Lichtman, R. R. (1985). Social comparison in adjustment to breast cancer. *Journal of Personality and Social Psychology, 49*, 1169–1183.

World Health Organization (2002, May 30). African AIDS Vaccine Programme Needs US $233 Million. Press Release WHO/42. Retrieved on June 11, 2002 from the Internet at http://www.who.int/inf/en/pr-2002-42.html

Wulfert, E., & Wan, C. K. (1995). Safer sex intentions and condom use viewed from a health belief, reasoned action, and social cognitive perspective. *The Journal of Sex Research, 32*, 299–311.

Yesmont, G. A. (1992). The relationship of assertiveness to college students' safer sex behaviors. *Adolescence, 27*, 253–272.

Author Index

Subject Index